100 DAYS TO
FREEDOM

from

Depression

Daily Devotional

STEPHEN ARTERBURN

AspirePress

100 Days to Freedom
from Depression

Published by Aspire Press
An imprint of Hendrickson Publishing Group
Rose Publishing, LLC
P.O. Box 3473
Peabody, Massachusetts 01961-3473 USA
www.HendricksonPublishingGroup.com

ISBN: 978-162862-997-2

Written with Anna Vaught

Book cover and layout design by Sergio Urquiza

Printed by APS
April 2021, 1st Printing

This book is given to

_____

on this day

_____

CONTENTS

Introduction

The National Institute of Mental Health defines depression as a "common but serious mood disorder that causes severe symptoms that affect how you feel, think, and handle daily activities, such as sleeping, eating, or working."[1]

Just like the flu, depression is not one size fits all. The sadness that one person feels is not the same darkness that another person feels. The pit of despair experienced by one is not the same well that another lives in. Consider:

- Depression is isolating. Depression is also a fake smile at a birthday party.

- Depression is exhaustion. Depression is also bursts of energy.

- Depression is crying. Depression is also laughing in an effort to fit in.

- Depression is agony. Depression is also leading what appears to be a normal functioning life.

- Depression is an internal battle. Depression is also the mask we wear.

- Depression is temporary. Depression seems like forever.

How do we deal with such a chameleon? How do we start to change how we think? The Bible is a great place to start. God's Word is more than a few feel-good sentences. It is living and breathing and has the power to change the heart and mind.

If you or someone you know is experiencing an emptiness that cannot be explained, diagnosed or undiagnosed, reach out for help. Make sure it is centered on the truths of God's Word.

DAY 1

God Beckons

Come to me, all you who labor and are heavy laden,
and I will give you rest.

MATTHEW 11:28 NKJV

When you read the above invitation, do any of these responses sound familiar:

- "I got it; I can manage."
- "If I ask for or receive help, I will be seen as weak."
- "That person has it worse than I do."

In a world where we're applauded for our independence, God's words can sound foreign. Furthermore, our experiences might have taught us to rely only on ourselves to make the best decisions we can, to trust our instincts as we try to survive all that life sends our way.

Depression or despondency can feel like a heavy blanket that weighs us down or a fog that prevents us from thinking clearly. We can feel helpless and alone to the point of hiding our true feelings for fear of being shamed or misunderstood. We try to figure it out. We reach for temporary fixes. We resort to anything that makes us feel better. But without appropriate care, we can spiral into hopelessness.

Jesus communicated the heaviness he felt in the garden of Gethsemane. In Matthew 26:37-38, he tells his friends how he feels and asks them to be with him. Then in Matthew 26:39, he reaches out to God—and God stood ready to give an answer. The rest of the story reveals that the God of heaven did not remove the events that caused Jesus' sorrow but instead was with Jesus every step. And he promises to be there to help us, too.

﹏

Those who are heavy-laden with despair should come unto the Lord.

Ezra Taft Benson

Draw aside, into the secret place no one but you and God can explore. This is a place from which all questions can be revered. Doubts and struggles are safe to open up and wrestle with, in this place. Tears are welcome.

Jenneth Graser

Any concern too small to be a prayer is too small to be a burden.

Corrie ten Boom

﹏

For Further Reflection

Psalm 34:17; Psalm 55:22; Isaiah 41:13

TODAY'S PRAYER

Father, I am sinking. Please help me to move toward the life preserver of your Word and your people to find rest. Give me the courage and strength to take the next step. Be the bright light on the path of my healing journey. Amen.

DAY 2

Have You Asked?

Share each other's burdens, and in this way
obey the law of Christ.

GALATIANS 6:2 NLT

So many of us live a life that is overflowing with things to do. It is not that those items are good or bad but rather just part of life. For example, we may be the head of a large project at work that requires lots of overtime; we may have children who are involved in sports and their final games are the same week; we might be dealing with a child who was sent home sick by the school nurse; and the car needs maintenance; and if we stop long enough, we may recognize we do not feel so good either. Just listing everything that can be on our plates is overwhelming!

But why do we try to manage everything by ourselves? Is it the belief that to be a "good Christian" we must do it all? Is it pride? Somewhere in our minds, we came to believe that sharing our needs with others is a sign that we are irresponsible, unorganized, unspiritual, not a good mother, father, sister, brother, aunt, uncle, etc. In this line of thinking, our accomplishment scale runs our lives.

Why are we like this? Maybe we don't want to be a burden or risk being rejected. Or we're skeptical about receiving help with no strings attached. Whatever the reason, doing life on our own and in our own strength is contrary to Scripture. In fact, God commands us to walk alongside each other (Galatians 6:2).

Asking for help is a sign of strength, not weakness. It shows humility rather than pride. Our help can come in two ways:

- From God himself, who is eager to respond to us (Isaiah 65:24) and is known in the Bible as our provider (*Jehovah-Jireh*).

- From other believers, who can help us experience the blessing of being in the family of God and looking out for each other (Philippians 2:4).

You are never strong enough that you don't need help.

César Chávez

If you are at a hard place in life, hesitant to ask for help, God invites you to ask him so he can meet your need.

David Jeremiah

For Further Reflection

Psalm 20:1; Psalm 91:15

TODAY'S PRAYER

God, I need you. I admit I've been trying to do life on my own. In my pride, I think I can manage everything coming my way, but I can't. Please help me to seek you for direction and practical support from other believers. Amen.

The Whole Temple

Do you not know that your bodies are temples of the Holy Spirit, who is in you, whom you have received from God? You are not your own; you were bought at a price. Therefore, honor God with your bodies.

1 Corinthians 6:19–20

Our bodies are amazing organisms—and God created them that way. The various parts and systems all connect and affect the others.

The Bible shows the value God puts on our bodies. The Holy Spirit lives in every believer. However, all too often we do not treat our bodies in a way that honors God. Our lifestyle and the choices we make can negatively affect our physical, spiritual, and emotional well-being.

- Let's begin to value our bodies in a way that pleases God.

- Let's become aware of what we put into our bodies, making healthy dietary and exercise choices.

- Let's start to pay attention to what we watch and listen to, focusing on things that are uplifting and beneficial.

- Let's recognize our emotions and feelings and engage in healthy relationships.

- Let's start having or renewing a regular time with God and fellow believers.

Taking these steps will lead to a more balanced life.

What is always speaking silently is the body.

Norman Brown

Bottom line, your body is a temple, and you have to treat it that way. That's how God designed it.

Ray Lewis

For Further Reflection

1 Corinthians 10:31; Philippians 4:8; Hebrews 10:25

TODAY'S PRAYER

Heavenly Father, thank you for the realization that my body is not my own. Please help me to make better choices and to be a good steward of my physical, spiritual, and emotional health. I live to give you glory. Amen.

Don't Give Up!

*Not only so, but we also glory in our suffering,
because we know that suffering produces perseverance;
perseverance, character; and character, hope.*

Romans 5:3–4

Illness of any kind is difficult, and long-term illness can threaten to overwhelm. The toll it takes on us, our family, and friends can be exhausting. We might do everything we can and still be left with no answer, no change, and no hope. Sometimes we question the providence of God. We ask, "If he is so good, how can this be happening?" We question whether he really does hear or answer prayer. With no answers, we may feel ignored or give up on God.

In the book of John, Jesus gives a farewell to the disciples the night before his crucifixion. He speaks about the work of the Holy Spirit, the trouble they will face, and the hope that is to come. In John 16:33, Jesus says, "I have told you these things, so that in me you may have peace. In this world you will have trouble. But take heart! I have overcome the world."

In this scripture, Jesus acknowledges the hardships of life, but he wants his disciples to remember his words when they came against difficulties, opposition, and failures. He called them—as he calls us—to persevere, remembering that through him, there is victory. And through perseverance, we will develop character and hope.

You may be dealing with a recent diagnosis or a lifelong illness. You may be ready to stop trusting and waiting on

God to bring the healing. The challenge is to accept the situation with the assurance that God already has the victory over it.

Long-lasting victory can never be separated from a long-lasting stand on the foundation of the cross.

Watchman Nee

It always seems impossible until it's done.

Nelson Mandela

Most of the important things in the world have been accomplished by people who have kept on trying when there seemed to be no hope at all.

Dale Carnegie

For Further Reflection

Romans 12:12; Philippians 1:2-6; 2 Thessalonians 3:13

TODAY'S PRAYER

Heavenly Father, lead me through the trials I face today. Please give me everything I need to walk the path you have laid out for me. Remind me that I am not alone in this. I don't know your plan, but I know your plan is perfect. Amen.

God in the Valley

Behold, I am with you and will keep you wherever you go, and will bring you back to this land. For I will not leave you until I have done what I have promised you.

GENESIS 28:15 ESV

Nothing compares to being on a mountaintop. In the literal sense, everywhere we look, we see the skies above and vivid colors of the earth below. The sunrise and sunset can be breathtaking, and all feels right with the world. We might feel spiritually in tune, with God at the forefront of our minds. We praise and thank him for blessing us. We trust him and feel secure.

At other times, life throws us circumstances that can surprise and shake us. Negative thoughts and feelings invade. Fear. Sadness. Irritability. Anxiety. When negative emotions take the lead, we have to refocus, remembering that the God of the good times has not left us in the turbulent ones.

God is never off duty, never misses an event, and is never surprised (Psalm 121:4). So why is it that when we're on a mountaintop, we can praise God, but when we're in the valley, we wonder where he went? Maybe because:

- We lose our focus, we can become so overwhelmed and distracted by our challenges that we stop talking to God.

- We are disappointed with God, we mistakenly assume that bad things don't happen to Christians.

- We forget our blessings, we don't call to mind the things God has already done for us and in us.

Throughout the Bible we read of God's people being joyful and praising him when circumstances were going well, then struggling and doubting God when they weren't. Victory in the valley happened for those who remembered that God was still with them, and who sought his face even when things looked their worst.

God, who is everywhere, never leaves us. Yet he seems sometimes to be present, sometimes to be absent. If we do not know him well, we do not realize that he may be more present to us when he is absent than when he is present.

Thomas Merton

The hilltop hour would not be half so wonderful if there were no dark valleys to traverse.

Helen Keller

Mountains, hills and valleys confirm the beauty of your holiness.

Euginia Herlihy

For Further Reflection

Psalm 121:1–2; Jonah 2:6; Isaiah 41:10

TODAY'S PRAYER

Lord, thank you for meeting me exactly where I am. Please help me to keep my eyes focused on you as you guide me on a path forward. Amen.

Walking Through

When you pass through the waters, I will be with you;
and through the rivers, they shall not overwhelm you;
when you walk through fire you shall not be burned,
and the flame shall not consume you.

Isaiah 43:2 ESV

Sometimes we might find ourselves stuck in a place we don't want to be and don't know how to get out of. Maybe we've reached out and tried to make changes or find a better path, only to end up back in the same place, day after day, feeling discouraged.

Times of struggle, grief, or need can leave us feeling unsure and fearful. But Psalm 23:4 boasts this comforting statement: "Even though I walk through the valley of the shadow of death, I will fear no evil, for you are with me; your rod and your staff, they comfort me" (ESV).

When children are exploring, sometimes they walk, grab, open, and push everything as their curiosity gets the best of them. Other times—when they don't dare go alone—they reach for the finger of someone bigger to join them in their discovery. And with that grip secure, they can do anything.

Similarly, in times of fear or uncertainty, God offers his saving hands for us to hold. He will walk with—even sometimes carry—us through the shadowy places. We have the promise of a God who will join us for the journey. We can rest in the knowledge that he holds our past, present, and future.

In the end, if we don't have God, we don't have anything other than an end.

Craig D. Lounsbrough

God never said that the journey would be easy, but he did say that the arrival would be worthwhile.

Max Lucado

For Further Reflection

Deuteronomy 31:8; Isaiah 45:2

TODAY'S PRAYER

Father, thank you for the promise that you will be with me always. As I walk through these dark days, I know you see me, but sometimes I can't see you. I can't sense you. Help me to reach out to your mighty finger that will never let me go. Amen.

Embracing Weakness

*But he said to me, "My grace is sufficient for you,
for My power is made perfect in weakness."
Therefore I will boast all the more gladly about my
weaknesses, so that Christ's power may rest on me.*

2 CORINTHIANS 12:9

We live in a world where the norm is for everyone to share their strengths and accomplishments. The focus is on what we have mastered or conquered. Even when we're asked to share our weaknesses, we often frame it in a way that makes us look good. For example:

Interviewer question: "What is your greatest weakness?"

Interviewee response: "I'm a perfectionist."

That answer might land you the job, but what about other situations in life? What about times when we're struggling spiritually yet shy away from being honest? Consider this scenario:

Friend 1: "I'm so sorry to hear about your diagnosis. How can I pray for you?"

Friend 2: "Praise the Lord, God is good. We're fine. Just pray for peace and patience as I trust in his timing for a cure."

On the surface, that might sound like a good answer. But what if:

Friend 2: "I've been praying to God for healing but he's silent. I'm losing faith that God will ever heal me. I can't worship. I can't even pray."

This type of response cannot be spun as a strength. It's authentic and reveals the pain and hurt. We might give canned answers to hide our pain from others, but God knows what we're going through, and he knows our inmost thoughts.

In our struggle, pain, or discomfort, our relationship with the Lord can grow and reshape how we live our lives. In our greatest weaknesses and failings, God shows redemption and grace. How wonderful it is to be able to acknowledge our ugliest thoughts and feelings before God, and let his Spirit heal our hearts and his power transform our lives.

The Christian thinks his weaknesses are his greatest hindrance in the life and service of God; God tells us that it is the secret of strength and success. It is our weakness, heartily accepted and continually realized, that gives our claim and access to the strength of him who has said, "My strength is made perfect in weakness."

Andrew Murray

Real true faith is man's weakness leaning on God's strength.

Dwight L. Moody

Deny your weakness, and you will never realize God's strength in you.

Joni Eareckson Tada

For Further Reflection

1 Samuel 16:7; Psalm 46:1; Romans 8:26

TODAY'S PRAYER

Father, thank you that I can be real with you. Thank you that my authenticity with you and people who truly care for me will not result in abandonment but rather an opportunity to watch you work in my weakness. Help me to remember that when I'm weak, I'm open to your strength. Amen.

Outside the Box

[Jesus] said to Simon, "Put out into deep water, and let down the nets for a catch." Simon answered, "Master, we've worked hard all night and haven't caught anything. But because you say so, I will let down the nets."

LUKE 5:1–5

God often acts in ways that make no sense to us. We think we need to take the left fork in the road, and he takes us to the right. We might think our way is best, based on our knowledge and experiences. If it were up to us, we'd do things the way we always have, even if it causes pain.

Pause and read Luke 5:1-5 through three different lenses: First, consider the boat and the fishermen. It was inconvenient for Simon to loan his boat to Jesus. Why? The boat was not ready. The fishing day had ended, and Simon and his peers were washing their nets and putting their gear away. Second, the Bible says Peter and his coworkers were tired. They had worked all night. According to National Geographic, a fishing net can weigh ten to fifteen pounds when it's empty and can exceed 100 pounds when full.[2] Yet despite the disciples' fatigue, Jesus was calling them to try one more thing. Third, the disciples hadn't caught any fish. These professional fishermen had been unsuccessful in delivering the goods. Jesus was challenging their sense of expertise and demonstrating what can happen when situations—even failures—are left in his hands.

Maybe you've done everything you know how to do to and haven't found victory. But maybe you sense God asking you to put aside your know-how and try one more time ... his way. Let down your net and get ready for a catch.

Normality is a paved road. It's comfortable to walk, but no flowers grow on it.

Vincent van Gogh

God has wonderful plans for you—if you let him lead and comfort.

Colin McCartney

When you have exhausted all possibilities, remember this: you haven't.

Thomas Edison

For Further Reflection

Luke 5:1-11; 1 Corinthians 2:13; Isaiah 55:8-9

TODAY'S PRAYER

Father, please forgive me for the times I ignored your prompts and proceeded using my own understanding and my own will. Please give me the courage to let down my net again. Amen.

Don't Go It Alone

Two are better than one, because they have a good
return for their labor: If either of them falls down,
one can help the other up. But pity anyone
who falls and has no one to help them up.

ECCLESIASTES 4:9–10

In a world with approximately 7.8 billion people, it can be easy to say we are not alone. But how many of us live in community with real connections to others?

Some of us are led to believe we are surrounded by friends because of how many "followers," "likes," or "friend requests" we have on social media. Even our interactions with coworkers and neighbors might remain superficial. If we are not cognizant of our behaviors, our relationships at church can have the same tone. A lot of us might show up for the sermon, sliding in at the last minute and skipping out before the closing prayer. Others might visit many churches, never committing to grow and invest in one congregation—or limiting involvement to being a spectator. But when a need comes up, or when we start to drift spiritually, we have few people around to offer support or accountability. We've put ourselves in a situation where we're on our own.

What comes to mind when you think about living in a safe, biblical community? For some of us, our hearts just skipped a beat and anxiety is creeping in at the thought of letting down our guard and trusting others. But God's desire for us is to invest in each other's lives. God intended for us to live in community—connected to people who look out for one another. Being connected allows us to let our guard down, develop trust, and be known. Even though our world sends the message to "do you," God's Word tells us we function better in a tribe. There is safety in numbers.

We weren't created to be independent, autonomous, or self-sufficient. We were made to live in a humble, worshipful, and loving dependency upon God and in a loving and humble interdependency with others.

Paul Tripp

Alone we can do so little; together we can do so much.

Helen Keller

It takes two flints to make a fire.

Louisa May Alcott

For Further Reflection

Genesis 2:18; 1 Thessalonians 5:14;
1 Corinthians 12:25-27

TODAY'S PRAYER

Father, you created me for connection. I pray you open my eyes to opportunities for real relationships—community where I can give and receive. Amen.

Balm

But I will restore to you your health
and heal your wounds.

JEREMIAH 30:17

We know the general rules for good physical health: eat right, drink plenty of water, get enough rest, and exercise. But even if we keep all the rules, we'll still get sick. Some of us might carry the burden of a chronic physical illness. When we're physically ill, we seek the advice of a physician.

We have the same basic rules for good mental health: eat right, drink plenty of water, get enough rest, and exercise. But even if we keep all the rules, we might experience some type of mental health issue. But for some reason, some people believe the misconception that mental health issues are simply a spiritual health issue, and no physician can help.

Consider this: physicians and the medicine they prescribe are a blessing from God. The Old Testament refers to physicians as servants (Genesis 50:2), performing surgical procedures that are used at God's command (Genesis 17:10-14). Proverbs 17:22 states that medicine can improve a person's countenance. The New Testament echoes the sentiment with Jesus declaring the sick need a physician (Luke 5:31). Additionally, one of the Gospel writers, Luke, was a physician (Colossians 4:14).

God is the Great Physician. He alone understands how our body, mind, and soul work together. So why do we sometimes hesitate to seek help for our mental or spiritual challenges?

Whether the illness is physical or mental, healing comes from God, and he might use a person or medicine to accomplish his will. We might never know why some people experience a miraculous healing and others continue to search for relief. But with God as our strength, we can surrender, letting him do his work, his way, in his time.

There is a balm in Gilead, to make the wounded whole; there's power enough in heaven, to cure the sin-sick soul.

African American Spiritual

His presence was somehow a balm on the open wound of my heart.

Jasinda Wilder

For Further Reflection

2 Kings 20:7; Matthew 9:12; Revelation 22:2

TODAY'S PRAYER

Father, thank you for the men and women you have gifted to develop the many balms that bring some relief to many diseases. Please direct me in the ways I should go regarding physicians and medicines. I continue to pray for my healing whether through your divine work or a doctor. Amen.

Perfectionism

*I do not consider myself yet to have taken hold of it.
But one thing I do: Forgetting what is behind
and straining toward what is ahead, I press on
toward the goal to win the prize for which God
has called me heavenward in Christ Jesus.*

PHILIPPIANS 3:13–14

Striving for excellence is generally an acceptable way to live life. We strive for excellence in school because our efforts might result in a reward that will help with our future education. We pursue excellence at work to advance in our field. And when we fail, many of us simply learn and move on. However, if we start shifting toward perfectionism, we can find ourselves headed down an unhealthy path.

Perfectionism is two sides of the same coin. On one side, perfectionistic traits can help us be deliberate and methodical in how we live. On the other side, those perfectionistic traits can make us overly critical and unforgiving of ourselves when we make a mistake. We run the scenario through our minds, analyzing and reanalyzing our behaviors, trying to identify the one area that caused us to miss the mark. We compare ourselves to others, always trying to be the best. We might lack the flexibility to try a different route. Staying on this path can bring us to a place of regret, despondency, and depression.

In God's family, we are accepted as is, with all our flaws and shortcomings. He does not require us to be perfect. God invites us to take our eyes off ourselves and fix them on him—the only One who is perfect. Then we are free to pursue godly things, knowing that when we make a mistake, Jesus has already forgiven and will restore us.

The goal is excellence (in his name), not perfection.

We are not called to pursue perfection; we're called to pursue Christ, who is perfect.

Shelia Walsh

God is looking for imperfect men and women who have learned to walk in moment-by-moment dependence on the Holy Spirit. Christians who have come to terms with their inadequacies, fears, and failures. Believers who have become discontent with "surviving" and have taken the time to investigate everything God has to offer in this life.

Charles Stanley

Imperfections are not inadequacies; they are reminders that we're all in this together.

Brené Brown

For Further Reflection

2 Peter 1:3; 2 Corinthians 10:12

TODAY'S PRAYER

Father, you are the only one who is perfect. I ask that you send your Holy Spirit to help liberate me the performer, the perfectionist. Help me to see myself as you see me. And give me the grace to see others as you see them. Amen.

In Tune with Our Bodies

Dear friend, I pray that you may enjoy good health and that all may go well with you, even as your soul is getting along well.

3 JOHN 1:2

The human body is a work of art (Psalm 139:13). The Artist spent intentional time designing each limb, each hair, each organ, each artery, each vein. The way the body parts function together and separately is a feat the best engineers can only attempt to achieve.

After the introduction of sin in the garden of Eden, the ability for our bodies to operate in perfection was lost. Whether it's the normal passage of time or the way in which we've treated our body, our systems will decline.

Living the full life God intended will include paying attention to our bodies. Even without a medical degree, we can notice if something seems "off." Some things to consider may include: any unusual external changes (i.e. bug bite); sleeping or eating more (or less); just not feeling like yourself.

These are just a few occurrences we may notice about ourselves, but sometimes we are too close to see everything. We can also rely on those closest to us to point out where we do not seem like ourselves. Armed with observations and feedback, we can begin to explore with the right person what may be causing disharmony in our bodies.

God wants us to treat our bodies well. When we care for all aspects of his masterpiece, God can use us to our fullest because we have the energy we need for his work. When we neglect our bodies, we are not equipped to live the life God has for us and we can be missing out on blessings.

God made your body, Jesus died for your body, and he expects you to take care of your body.

Rick Warren

Our bodies are our gardens, to the which our wills are gardeners.

William Shakespeare

Health is not valued till sickness comes.

Thomas Fuller

For Further Reflection

Psalm 139:13–18; Proverbs 3:1–2; 1 Corinthians 15:44

TODAY'S PRAYER

Father, I thank you that I am fearfully and wonderfully made. I am unique by design and your fingerprint is on me. Help me to take care of your masterwork for your glory. Amen.

Finding Hope

And now, O Lord, for what do I wait? My hope is in you.

PSALM 39:7 ESV

Those suffering from depression search for relief from its grip. Whether our experience is related to a loss or the unexplained sadness that takes over our lives, this emotional disease saps our ability to know what to do next. Our thinking can become unclear, and we can lose our ability to focus. Without some way to cope with what we feel, we can approach the abyss of hopelessness.

What is hope? Hope is the anchor of life. Hope is the unshakeable belief that things will get better. We have hope when we have proof that things are moving in the right direction, even if that movement seems small—so small it might take others to point it out to us.

What does hope look like with depression? Hope is that we will start to feel better. That we'll start to feel excitement about the simple things in life again. Hope is the realization that we will make it through. Hope is different from a wish. Hope is not necessarily rooted in something tangible; it's a reaction to the smallest thing that intersects our path and turns us toward healing.

For those who believe in the Lord Jesus Christ, our best hope is him and that he can make all things right. Take time to look at the Bible stories that demonstrate hope in the "For Further Reflection" reading. Each person in those stories knew something about Jesus' teaching and miracles. Each story also highlights unhesitating hope in Jesus' ability to heal. Whether it be a touch or a word, Jesus can make all things right.

Depression might make us feel that we have lost everything, but with hope we have everything.

Hope begins in the dark, the stubborn hope that if you just show up and try to do the right thing, the dawn will come. You wait and watch and work: you don't give up.

Anne Lamott

Without Christ there is no hope.

Charles Spurgeon

True faith means holding nothing back. It means putting every hope in God's fidelity to his Promises.

Francis Chan

For Further Reflection

Luke 7:1-10; Luke 8:41-56

TODAY'S PRAYER

Thank you Father that you are victorious over everything. When life turns dark, and I have turned over every stone, help me to remember that my hope is in you. And because of who you are, I can walk in victory. Amen.

Speechless

In all their distress he too was distressed, and the
angel of his presence saved them. In his love
and mercy he redeemed them; he lifted them
up and carried them all the days of old.

ISAIAH 63:9

If someone has never suffered from depression, it might be difficult for that person to imagine feeling weak and lonely. Those close to us try to understand and offer comfort, but their words often rebound off the barrier of depression, leaving us feeling separated from them.

Depression can create the sense of being alone, especially when there seems to be no one who understands how we feel. Our pain is not something that can be seen, or corrected with a bandage or cast. We might try to explain what we believe is going on in our bodies and minds, but depression can be perplexing, even to ourselves. How do we explain what is happening when we don't fully understand? The inability to communicate effectively can leave us feeling more isolated, with nowhere to turn.

If people around us—people we can see—can't understand what we're going through, what about God, whom we can't see? The Bible encourages us to bring our heart's desires to God. But what happens when we have no words?

The good news is that the Lord "gets it." God understands what we need—even when we cannot speak. Romans 8:26 says the Holy Spirit will help us when we are at our weakest, and when we do not have the words, he will speak for us "with groanings too deep for words" (ESV). When we are feeble, he is there, giving us what we need to take the next step. And the next. And we can keep relying on him for the steps to come. He will carry us through.

God gets it. When you reach out to Him, he is not looking for fancy words that would impress your English teacher. He sees your heart. A groan, a look, a sigh—he speaks every language. He understands.

Max Lucado

Groanings which cannot be uttered are often prayers which cannot be refused.

Charles Spurgeon

Prayer requires more of the heart than of the tongue.

Adam Clarke

For Further Reflection

Deuteronomy 1:31; Deuteronomy 32:11

TODAY'S PRAYER

Heavenly Father, help me to remember your promises—that you are always with me and you know me. Help me to remember to reach out to you when I have no words, knowing that you hear me. Amen.

The Day Is Coming

*I wait for the LORD, my soul waits. And in his word
I do hope. My soul waits for the LORD more
than those who watch for the morning.*

PSALM 130:5–6 NKJV

Life is full of anticipation, times spent waiting for something to arrive or happen. Our minds play the upcoming event on repeat. We look forward to that day, preparing and waiting, wondering what it will be like. Then it happens! The day arrives, and we feel a sense relief and excitement. Our stomachs flutter a bit. Our hearts race a little faster. Our eyes widen, a smile appears, and every trouble or concern seems to fade in comparison to the arrival of the moment we've been waiting for.

Do you remember the last time you felt this way? Well, another day like that is coming. During times of trial, it might be hard to know it's true. So much might be clouding our vision that it's difficult to see anything. And for some of us, we have been waiting expectantly for a long time. Maybe we've been waiting for a reprieve or cure or simply a change for the better that never seems to come. Instead, we're living with a body or mind that—in our belief—has failed us. All our tears, prayers, interventions have yielded no relief. We are done! But God is not.

God never promised a life without pain or discomfort. However, his Word does declare that at his designated time, all agony, worries, and hurt will be no more. He will gather us into his arms and wipe away our tears. The trial will be over. And that is worth waiting for.

True worship is open to God, adoring God, waiting for God, trusting God even in the dark.

N. T. Wright

Waiting for God means power to do nothing save under command. This is not lack of power to do anything. Waiting for God needs strength rather than weakness. It is power to do nothing. It is the strength that holds strength in check. It is the strength that prevents the blundering activity which is entirely false and will make true activity impossible when the definite command comes.

G. Campbell Morgan

If the Lord Jehovah makes us wait, let us do so with our whole hearts; for blessed are all they that wait for Him. He is worth waiting for. The waiting itself is beneficial to us: it tries faith, exercises patience, trains submission, and endears the blessing when it comes. The Lord's people have always been a waiting people.

Charles Spurgeon

For Further Reflection

Psalm 62:6; Mark 13:32; Matthew 5:4

TODAY'S PRAYER

Lord, I know you have a timing for everything. While I wait to be healed, please help me to expect to see you in every day of my life, until I see you face to face. Amen.

Persevering in the Present

He will wipe every tear from their eyes. There will be
no more death or mourning or crying or pain,
for the old order of things has passed away.

REVELATION 21:4

At times, we all have difficult experiences that never seem to end. Despite our best plans, we are unable to change paths and improve our circumstances, which leaves us frustrated. This feels especially poignant for those of us who struggle with depression.

Everyone is susceptible to distress. We live in a fallen world where our bodies are not invincible. Some distress lasts only a short period. We follow the prescription, and we are cured. Other illnesses don't go away. We are left with feelings of fear, anxiety, and or sadness about the future.

Living with a chronic distress state can be overwhelming, and we might be tempted to substitute thriving for existing. The truth is, we might not be healed on this side of heaven. But the book of Revelation gives a glimpse of what life will be like after we die. A day is coming when our loving Father will make all things right. Our tears will stop because there will be no more pain. The sadness that hung over us for a time will be no more.

In this life, we might never understand the *why* behind our suffering, but we should never forget we serve a God whose thoughts and ways are above ours (Isaiah 55:8-9). His vision and plan for us is broader than our limited view and comprehension. Though our eyes might be looking expectantly to the blessings of the future, we can also find joy and peace in the present, resting in the knowledge that our all-knowing and compassionate Father is right here with us.

God is never late and rarely early. He is always exactly right on time—his time.

Dillon Burroughs

Sometimes arriving too quickly is detrimental. It is dangerous to arrive without our character mature or intact.

Lisa Bevere

To wait on God means to pause and soberly consider our own inadequacy and the Lord's all-sufficiency, and to seek counsel and help from the Lord, and to hope in Him. ... The folly of not waiting for God is that we forfeit the blessing of having God work for us.

John Piper

For Further Reflection

Proverbs 16:9; Galatians 5:22; James 1:4

TODAY'S PRAYER

Lord, it's hard to understand why life happens the way that it does. While I don't understand everything, I do understand that when you come again, everything will be made right and whole, including me. Thank you for that promise! Amen.

Gratitude

*Give thanks in all circumstances; for this
is the will of God in Christ Jesus for you.*

1 THESSALONIANS 5:18 ESV

Many times this verse is misquoted as "give thanks *for* all things." Think of it! Being grateful for the flat tire on the way to work; thankful for that argument with your spouse that left you with hurt feelings; thankful for the flu that touched everyone in your household. Is this proof that God is asking too much?

But what is he really asking? To give thanks *in* all circumstances. That sounds different—but maybe just as hard. When we are faced with heartache, disappointments, or loss, it can be easier to focus on what we do not have, or the ways events did not turn out as we expected. It can be easy to slip into trying to manipulate circumstances in our favor. The problem is that our view is short-sighted. We stop seeking God's will. Our focus is turned inward ... and limited.

What God is inviting us to do in times of distress is to turn our focus to him and the blessings he has provided. When we refocus, we realize that God has been faithful in the past and continues to be in the present. We start to remember that he has demonstrated his faithfulness in both good times and bad. When we focus on being grateful, the suffering and pain of today starts to shrink in comparison to what we know God can do. Our trust can grow and our anxiety lessen. Our mood can become more joyous and turn to praise and thanksgiving rather than complaint.

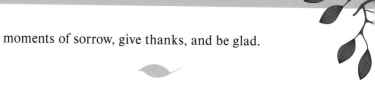

In moments of sorrow, give thanks, and be glad.

Gratitude ... makes sense of our past, brings peace for today, and creates a vision for tomorrow.

Melody Beattie

It is only with gratitude that life becomes rich.

Dietrich Bonhoeffer

Reflect upon your present blessings, of which every man has plenty; not on your past misfortunes, of which all men have some.

Charles Dickens

For Further Reflection

Psalm 118:24; Colossians 3:15; Psalm 103:2–5

TODAY'S PRAYER

Father, although I am struggling, I am willing to be grateful *in* my circumstances. Please help me to find something to be grateful for every day. Help me to see what I have instead of what I do not have. Amen.

Change Your Mind!

Do not conform any longer to the pattern of this world
but be transformed by the renewing of your mind.
Then you will be able to test and approve what
God's will is—his good, pleasing and perfect will.

ROMANS 12:2

Many of us spend much of our lives trying to prevent physical health issues. At the first symptoms, we quickly engage in self-care. We develop a plan we believe will reverse or perhaps stop the progression of the disease. So why do we treat instances of emotional distress differently?

People suffering from any type of emotional distress are often stigmatized. Because of this stigma, we think we cannot share for fear of being misunderstood and rejected. We might be struggling to accept a reality we cannot explain with words. The way we think about ourselves affects our behavior.

As believers, we must continually renew our minds so that we're thinking according to God's truth. The Bible often refers to the power of our minds and our thoughts. We have a choice between healthy thoughts that bring life or unhealthy thoughts that bring negativity and harm. It can be hard to reign in our thoughts. But we can make the conscious effort to pay attention to where a certain line of thought is taking us. Reframing our thoughts about our mental struggles will change our behavior regarding the treatment of our ailment. The Bible says this is possible.

God is with us and ready to help us capture our thoughts. When we recognize and change our negative thoughts about ourselves and our struggles, we are opening ourselves up to the love and support God has for us from him and from other believers.

The mind can descend far lower than the body, for in it there are bottomless pits. The flesh can bear only a certain number of wounds and no more, but the soul can bleed in ten thousand ways, and die over and over again each hour.

Charles Spurgeon

As you pray for the Holy Spirit to make you aware of thoughts that come into your mind that don't line up with God's Word, you'll begin to realize when those thoughts come and you can renew your mind with the Word.

Joyce Meyer

God desires to change us from the inside out. Renewing our minds, starving our self-destructive tendencies, and teaching us to form new habits.

Beth Moore

For Further Reflection

Philippians 4:8; 2 Corinthians 10:5

TODAY'S PRAYER

Father, thank you for making me the way I am. You know my thoughts. You know when they align with your thoughts and when they don't. Teach me to recognize when I am not thinking of myself the way you do. Amen.

Serving Others

*Whoever wants to be my disciple must deny themselves
and take up their cross and follow me. For whoever wants
to save their life will lose it, but whoever loses their life
for me will find it. What good will it be for someone
to gain the whole world, yet forfeit their soul?*

MATTHEW 16:24–26

Depression can be debilitating. Sadness can linger for days, weeks, or months. We might lose interest in activities we used to enjoy. Sometimes we experience physical changes, such as a change in sleeping patterns.

Regardless of the symptoms and severity of depression, isolation is a common byproduct. Our tendency is to withdraw into ourselves and our struggles. However, the Bible talks extensively about how Christians should live with an outward focus—in love and service to others. When we are experiencing depression, it can be hard to follow *any* of God's directions, but if we act in obedience, even when we don't want to, God will bless us.

In today's scripture, Jesus said, "For whoever wants to save their life will lose it, but whoever loses their life for me will find it." Science supports these words. One study published in *Psychosomatic Medicine* revealed that giving outweighed receiving. The participants who gave to others experienced reduced stress levels and felt good.[3] Helping others ultimately helps you. In fact, an increasing number of studies being published show the positive effects of helping others. Research is not necessarily saying that serving is the cure, but perhaps it is a way to experience finding life again.

Those who are happiest are those who do the most for others.

Booker T. Washington

Life's most persistent and urgent question is: What are you doing for others?

Martin Luther King, Jr.

The only way you can serve God is by serving other people.

Rick Warren

For Further Reflection

Proverbs 19:17; Philippians 2:3–4; Galatians 5:13

TODAY'S PRAYER

Father, allow me to see outside my circumstances to serve others. Help me to find joy and peace in doing your work while you are working in me. Amen.

God Keeps You

To him who is able to keep you from stumbling
and to present you before his glorious presence
without fault and with great joy.

JUDE 24 NLT

We go to the doctor's office, take tests, and then we wait for results. Regardless of the outcome, we know that we will move forward into unchartered waters.

God's people consistently walked into the unknown. In Exodus, we read about God delivering the Hebrew people out of Egypt through Moses. It was an answer to prayer—until they realized they were being pursued by Pharaoh to the edge of the sea. Then God stepped in and parted the waters. Deuteronomy 29:5 states that after forty years on the journey, the Israelites' shoes and clothes did not wear out. Later, when Joshua prayed, asking God to give the army more light so they could see and destroy the enemy, God stopped the sun in the sky. Joshua 10:14 says, "There has never been a day like it before or since, a day when the LORD listened to a human being. Surely the LORD was fighting for Israel!"

God's people stepped out in faith not knowing what was coming next. Each time, God showed his power by providing everything they needed. God does the same for us. We might not know what an ailment will bring, but we do know a God who is with us for the journey, no matter what happens along the way.

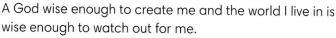

A God wise enough to create me and the world I live in is wise enough to watch out for me.

Philip Yancey

There is unspeakable comfort in knowing that God is constantly taking knowledge of me in love and watching over me for my good.

J. I. Packer

Wherever you go, God is with you—watching over you, protecting you, and providing the truth you need for every situation. The question is, will you open your heart to his Word, apply it to your life, and allow God to change you so that he can use you in ways far greater than you can imagine?

Charles Stanley

For Further Reflection

Philippians 4:19; Luke 12:24; Psalm 81:10

TODAY'S PRAYER

Father, my circumstances are uncertain. I do not have a clear direction. But I thank you that you already see the next steps and the outcome. Help me to find peace as I step out in faith. In Jesus' name.

Amen

DAY 21

Surprise!

Why, you do not even know what will happen tomorrow.
What is your life? You are a mist that appears for a little
while and then vanishes. Instead, you ought to say, "If it
is the Lord's will, we will live and do this or that."

JAMES 4:14–15

Spontaneity in life can be exciting. It can be fun to explore and discover new things, never knowing where we are going or what we will be doing. Other aspects of life tend to be planned. Appointments and phone calls can dictate what happens during the day. But sometimes life can take a turn that was not on the schedule. A failing grade. An illness. A job loss. An addition to the family.

In life, unexpected—and unfortunate—things often happen. They might not be caused by anything we, or anyone else, said or did. We live in a fallen world and life happens. However, we do not have to let this interruption sideline us. We have a choice: resist and fight the unexpected circumstance, or accept it and persevere.

To persevere, one of the first things we can do is stop, take a breather, and pray, so that we avoid reacting in an unbiblical way. We can take a moment to call on the God of the universe, remembering that he has not been blindsided. Then, take a moment to step back and look at the situation. What are the options? Should we ask someone we trust to consider the situation and offer advice? During this time, we continue to seek the Lord and see if he is leading us in a direction. Lastly, we do not ignore the unexpected situation we find ourselves dealing with. Ignoring or denying the situation can make things worse. Being active in working toward a solution is a productive and healthy response.

When life surprises, we can resist and possibly miss what God has for us, or accept the detour and face the new road with a sense of adventure with God.

The strength of patience hangs on our capacity to believe that God is up to something good for us in all our delays and detours.

John Piper

Each day holds a surprise. But only if we expect it can we see, hear, or feel it when it comes to us. Let's not be afraid to receive each day's surprise, whether it comes to us as sorrow or as joy. It will open a new place in our hearts, a place where we can welcome friends and celebrate more fully our shared humanity.

Henri Nouwen

For Further Reflection

Psalm 31:15; Proverbs 16:9

TODAY'S PRAYER

Father, as I embrace this surprise, help me to stay focused on you. Help me to relinquish any plans or ideas that do not match yours. Amen.

Listening to His Voice

My sheep listen to my voice; I know them, and they follow me. I give them eternal life, and they shall never perish; no one will snatch them out of my hand.

JOHN 10:27–28

As Christians, we face spiritual battles every day. One of the most difficult battlefields is in the realm of our minds. Satan loves to interfere with our lives and attack us through our thought lives. If he can get our minds off Christ, Satan can get us off track. Often his tactics are subtle. In the garden of Eden, he tempted Eve by asking her whether God really meant what he said and by throwing aspersions on God's character. Satan will often raise similar questions and doubts with us, figuratively whispering in our ear, tempting us to doubt God's Word, disobey his commands, and resist his leading in our lives.

How can we avoid being led astray? By staying close to our Shepherd. As we draw closer to him, listening to the instruction in his Word, we become more familiar with the sound of his voice and recognizing his leading in our lives. Our thoughts and wills become more closely aligned with his. We can stay close to God by: quieting our hearts; praying; asking him to reveal himself through his Word; reading his Word, underlining or highlighting what stands out; meditating (considering, contemplating) a verse or two, or a whole passage; and regularly attending a church where God's Word is faithfully taught.

As we listen and follow our Shepherd's voice, our thoughts and behaviors align with his purpose and we can grow in our walk with him.

As long as we let the Word of God be our only armor, we can look confidently into the future.

Dietrich Bonhoeffer

If the Lord be with us, we have no cause of fear. His eye is upon us, his arm over us, his ear open to our prayer—his grace sufficient, his promise unchangeable.

John Newton

For Further Reflection

Jeremiah 15:16; Romans 10:17; Hebrews 4:12

TODAY'S PRAYER

Father, help me to guard my eyes and ears and to focus on your voice leading and guiding me. Help me to take time each day in your Word so that I grow in your truths. Amen.

Connection

Be devoted to one another in love. Honor one another
above yourselves. Never be lacking in zeal, but keep
your spiritual fervor, serving the Lord. Be joyful in hope,
patient in affliction, faithful in prayer.

ROMANS 12:10–12

Relationships are hard. While they can bring many joys, they can sometimes bring much pain. Sometimes when we've been deeply hurt, we might feel the solution is to separate ourselves from *everyone*. But isolation leaves us vulnerable, because a primary component of our emotional health is our connection with other people.

In a study conducted at University of Michigan, Ann Arbor, researchers found that people with low social connection have a greater propensity toward obesity and high blood pressure than those with strong social connections. Conversely, the study showed that people with strong social connections have lower levels of depression and anxiety. They also have higher levels of self-esteem and empathy.[4]

So how do we tap into this benefit when we are depleted by depression or hurt?

First, we must find the people we can go deep with. We know Jesus had three to six close people in his life: Peter, James, John, Mary, Martha, and Lazarus. Jesus never pretended; he shared his deepest struggle with those close to him. He sought people he knew would try to support him during his darkest hour. Jesus took the risk to open himself to others, knowing he might be rejected. We can follow this example.

Being physically, mentally, and spiritually healthy is tied to connection with others. To find our tribe takes boldness and risk; however, the rewards last a lifetime.

A Christian fellowship lives and exists by the intercession of its members for one another, or it collapses.

Dietrich Bonhoeffer

They reminded me that Christianity isn't meant to simply be believed; it's meant to be lived, shared, eaten, spoken, and enacted in the presence of other people. They reminded me that, try as I may, I can't be a Christian on my own. I need a community. I need the church.

Rachel Held Evans

For Further Reflection

Hebrews 13:16; 1 Thessalonians 5:11; Matthew 7:12

TODAY'S PRAYER

Father, in my darkest hours, please give me the strength to reach out to others. Help me to be authentic and true about what is occurring in my life. And as others become available to me, help me to be available for them. Amen.

The Power of the Pen

*Thus says the LORD, the God of Israel: Write in a book
all the words that I have spoken to you.*

JEREMIAH 30:2 ESV

Some of the best parts of the Bible are the conversations David has with God in the Psalms. There, David pours out his anger, his confusion, his praises, and his struggles. As we read the Psalms, we can see a shift in his mood and his thinking.

Writing has long been a tool used in the mental health field to help clients express their thoughts. Writing is believed to provide benefits both short and long term. Scientific evidence supports the notion that using the left and right brain at the same time helps remove mental blocks, helps to clear the mind, and helps identify the root of the trouble. Additionally, journaling can help us better understand patterns in our thinking and reveal our feelings and desires.

Journaling might sound daunting, but it doesn't have to be. First, start small. Make the effort to spend five minutes a couple of days a week before bed, simply writing a few words about your feelings. There is no need to edit. No one is looking for proper sentences or the correct spelling and use of words. Just write what comes to mind.

Second, designate a writing space. As you get used to expressing yourself in writing, you might invest in a special notebook that sits by the bed or is small enough to carry with you. As you write about anger, sadness, and other painful emotions, the intensity of those feelings will start to decrease. As the tension decreases, you might feel calmer and have a better outlook.

David was no stranger to emotions. Throughout his life, he poured out his negative or questioning thoughts and feelings to God. Often before a psalm was over, he would interject a positive thought and a truth about God. David's writings reduced his stress, helped him think more clearly and brought him peace. Writing can do the same for us.

I can shake off everything as I write; my sorrows disappear, my courage is reborn.

Anne Frank

Write hard and clear about what hurts.

Ernest Hemingway

Whenever you are fed up with life, start writing: ink is the great cure for all human ills, as I have found out long ago.

C. S. Lewis

For Further Reflection

Proverbs 20:5; Psalm 56:8

TODAY'S PRAYER

Gracious Father, thank you for David's example of how it is okay to be honest in my writings to you. Please help me to use this tool to uncover my hidden thoughts, bitter words, and depleting emotions. I offer them all to you for healing. Amen.

Dance, Play, and Sing a Little Louder!

Praise him with tambourine and dancing;
Praise him with the stringed instruments and flute.

PSALM 150:4 NASB

If everything in the Bible is there for a purpose, we should not overlook the significance of the many biblical references to music. Music is universal and cultural. The Bible talks about playing instruments before battle, as part of celebrations, and in times of sadness. Sometimes music includes words, and other times it is just the instruments speaking.

Music moves us. It brings emotions deep within us to the surface. And by doing so, we can experience healing. Researchers from McGill University in Canada found that listening to music increases good chemicals in the brain.[5] While varying types of research continues to be conducted around depression and the brain, we cannot deny how music affects the brain.

Sometimes when we are struggling with a sickness or ailment, we might struggle to find the words to describe what we are experiencing. But music can help draw out the words and the emotions we are experiencing. It can even lift the mood of the depressed. Sometimes music has the ability to communicate more effectively, and the people of the Bible knew this. Throughout the Bible, we find references to music—not only God's people playing and singing for him, but God celebrating us (Zephaniah 3:17).

The next time depression begins to creep into life, consider putting on some worship music. Listen. Hear the harmonies. Play your own tune. Move your body in an act of worshipful dancing. Experience the presence of God through music.

Music can lift us out of depression or move us to tears— it is a remedy, a tonic, orange juice for the ear. But for many of my neurological patients, music is even more—it can provide access, even when no medication can, to movement, to speech, to life. For them, music is not a luxury, but a necessity.

Dr. Oliver Sacks

Dance is the hidden language of the soul.

Martha Graham

For Further Reflection

Psalm 100:1; Psalm 150:6; Habakkuk 3:17–18

TODAY'S PRAYER

Father, thank you for the example of different ways to express how we truly feel. When I cannot find the words, please remind me to listen to and sing songs of praise that will direct my heart to you. Amen.

Jehovah-Rapha

Many are the afflictions of the righteous,
but the LORD delivers him out of them all.

PSALM 34:19 ESV

Since the events in the garden, where Adam and Eve disobeyed God, our world has been broken. Each of us wrestles with all kinds of sin that comes from our hearts as we try to live life on our terms. Without an intervention, we will continue to look to ourselves as the one who can make things better and bring healing if we just do the next thing. However, the only path to true healing is through Jesus Christ. And healing is his specialty.

Throughout the Bible are references to the physical healings of God. For example:

- In Matthew 8, Jesus heals a man with leprosy.

- In Mark 1, Jesus cures Peter's mother-in-law.

- In John 9, Jesus heals a man who was born blind.

Everyone walks around with wounds that cannot be seen— spiritual or emotional scars that can run deeper than any physical wound. But the God who has the power to heal physical wounds also heals the hidden wounds. Here are some biblical examples:

- In Psalm 23, David acknowledges that God heals and restores his soul.

- In Matthew 8, Jesus heals two demoniacs.

- In John 14, Jesus senses and calms the disciples' worrisome thoughts.

God is aware of, and can heal, the wounds deep within us. To him, our emotional pain is just as valid as any physical pain. Remembering that our God is the Great Physician can fill us with hope as we wait on his timing. Our outlook becomes expectant, looking to *Jehovah-Rapha* ("The Lord Who Heals")—the one who holds our lives in his hands.

Healing rain is a real touch from God. It could be physical healing or emotional or whatever.

Michael W. Smith

Time doesn't heal all wounds; God heals wounds.

Pete Wilson

How sweet the name of Jesus sounds in a believer's ear! It soothes his sorrows, heals his wounds, and drives away his fear.

John Newton

For Further Reflection

Jeremiah 30:17; Isaiah 30:26; Psalm 103:3

TODAY'S PRAYER

Lord, help me to lean on you for the ultimate comfort. Whether I am healed in this life or the next, help me to put full trust in you. Please give me full confidence in your grace. Amen.

DAY 27

Jehovah-Shammah

*Go therefore and make disciples of all nations, baptizing
them in the name of the Father and of the Son and of
the Holy Spirit, teaching them to observe all that
I have commanded you. And behold, I am
with you always, to the end of the age.*

Matthew 28:19–20 esv

ometimes we might look at the tragedies of our
world and wonder, "If there is a God, where is he
today?" How can children be killed and no one held
accountable? Why does he allow natural disasters? Why do
so many people suffer from poverty and disease? A world so
full of suffering can make us question the nature of a "good"
God.

The Bible teaches that suffering exists because we live in a
fallen world. The book of Job is one of the clearest examples
of suffering of the innocent. Job was a rich man with a large
family. The first verse describes him as "blameless" and
"upright" (Job 1:1). Through a series of events, God allowed
Satan to take everything from Job, including his health. Job
went through all the religious traditions of mourning. His
friends even joined him, appearing to offer help and counsel,
but in reality simply assigning blame to Job. Eventually, Job
demanded an audience with God to get an explanation for
what he was enduring. In the middle of Job's friends giving
speeches and advice, God interrupted.

God answered Job by showing up! That is all. God offered
no explanation about Job's tragedies. God simply stated the
facts of his character, his ability, and his deeds since the

beginning of time. Job quickly realized he was out of his depth. Listening to God reminded Job that even though he could not see God, the Lord of heaven was there. Through all the losses, through the vexing counsel of Job's friends, and all the way through Job's restoration, God is Jehovah-Shammah—"The Lord My Companion."

The God who was there for Job is the same God who is always with us.

God, who is everywhere, never leaves us. Yet he seems sometimes to be present, sometimes to be absent. If we do not know him well, we do not realize that he may be more present to us when he is absent than when he is present.

Thomas Merton

The Lord watches over us every moment of every day. He is there—and he cares—about every step and every breath.

Dillon Burroughs

For Further Reflection

Deuteronomy 31:8; Psalm 46:1; Exodus 33:14

TODAY'S PRAYER

Father, please help me to remember that you are always with me. Even when I don't "feel" your presence, please help me to remember the promises in your Word. Thank you that you will never leave me. Amen.

An Altered Perspective

While Paul was waiting for them in Athens,
he was deeply troubled by all the idols he saw
everywhere in the city. ... So Paul, standing
before the council, addressed them.

ACTS 17:16, 22 NLT

When it comes to addressing mental health challenges, we often think of eating better, getting more exercise, and finding professional help. But one technique is often left off the list: changing our mind-set.

None of us has control over every event that comes into our lives, but we do have a choice in how we approach it and work through it. We can concentrate on the negative and unpleasant and be upset about the detour to our plans, or we can choose to look for what God would have us see and do in the moment. We can change our perspective.

When Paul was waiting for Timothy and Silas in Athens, the rampant idolatry upset him. Given his recent beating and imprisonment in another city, Paul could have chosen to hide out in Athens in fear, looking out for his own safety and waiting in silence until his friends arrived. Instead, Paul looked at the situation through God's eyes and saw people in need. He used the Athenians' religious zeal as a connecting point for him to talk about the one true God (Acts 17:16–34).

The same shift in perspective can happen for us. No one would volunteer to struggle with a mental illness. But what if the things God wants us to accomplish are only possible through the struggle of depression?

Setting aside a few minutes every day to step back and consider emotional health from a different standpoint probably will not come naturally. But if we can look intentionally at the situation with a different lens, we can find acceptance while we persevere.

When we are no longer able to change a situation, we are challenged to change ourselves.

Viktor Frankl

If you don't like something change it; if you can't change it, change the way you think about it.

Mary Engelbreit

Perspective is everything when you are experiencing the challenges of life.

Joni Eareckson Tada

For Further Reflection

Colossians 3:2; Isaiah 55:8-9; 2 Peter 3:8-9

TODAY'S PRAYER

Jesus, sometimes my life seems chaotic. Sometimes I don't understand my path or your plans. Please remind me that you know every step I take and every situation I find myself in. Help me to see my days through your lens. Amen.

The Peace of God

*And the peace of God, which transcends all
understanding, will guard your hearts and
your minds in Christ Jesus.*

PHILIPPIANS 4:7

Our world history is full of stories of people on the hunt for peace. Some people, convinced that if they could conquer their enemy they would have peace, led wars that dragged on for years. Some people are convinced that if they acquire enough money, find fame, or marry the right person, they will finally be at peace. But the Bible tells us that true peace can't be found in earthly things. When our worlds have turned upside down through tragedy or illness and all worldly assurances fail, God's peace remains steadfast.

Isaiah 54:10 says, "'Though the mountains be shaken and the hills be removed, yet my unfailing love for you will not be shaken nor my covenant of peace be removed,' says the LORD, who has compassion on you." These words remind us that even when everything is falling apart and we are powerless, God's peace remains. This verse is a declaration and a promise. When we focus on God, our turbulent times fade in comparison (Isaiah 26:3).

Some of the heroes of the Bible at times appeared on the brink of devastation or annihilation, surrounded by their enemies or a sickness. Some of them at first approached their situation with human reasoning and worldly tactics and met with failure. But when they turned their focus to God and surrendered, they were able to press on through the trial, rising above the circumstances around them.

Peace is a gift from God, given to believers simply because of who God is and what Jesus Christ did for us. The promise of peace is ours for the asking.

Never be afraid to trust an unknown future to a known God. Jesus did not promise to change the circumstances around us. He promised great peace and pure joy to those who would learn to believe that God actually controls all things.

Corrie ten Boom

Because of the empty tomb, we have peace. Because of his resurrection, we can have peace during even the most troubling of times because we know he is in control of all that happens in the world.

Paul Chappell

If God be our God, he will give us peace in trouble. When there is a storm without, he will make peace within. The world can create trouble in peace, but God can create peace in trouble.

Thomas Watson

For Further Reflection

Numbers 6:24–26; Proverbs 3:5; John 14:27

TODAY'S PRAYER

Loving Father, please give me calm and peace in the middle of my storm. My ground is shaky, but I know you are my steady rock. Help me to remember what you have done in my past so I can move into my future with you. Amen.

Persist in the Silence

Will You do nothing after seeing these things, O Lord?
Will You keep quiet and make us suffer even more?

ISAIAH 64:12 NLV

Sometimes God seems silent. We find ourselves in a trial and feel we've done everything we're supposed to do, yet when we cry out to God, we hear no answer in return.

In the book of Job we read about a man whose life was disrupted by a series of tragedies. Job went to God, cried out, and asked for an explanation. He kept asking for thirty-seven chapters.

Some of us can relate. We have asked God for any number of things, but he doesn't seem to hear us. We might think he is ignoring us, and we wonder why. Maybe our requests don't seem at all extravagant. Maybe they're practical—a financial need, an employment need, a need for healing. Why would God be silent for those types of requests? If we are not careful, we can start to doubt God can and will provide or that there is a God. How can we avoid those traps? Some suggestions:

- Look inward. What is my motive for making this request? Is there anything or any person I want more than I want God?

- Accept that God is sovereign. God does not owe us an explanation.

- Listen for God. Has he already answered? Maybe we did not hear him or like his response.

- Keep asking, but do so with a surrendered heart. Job was persistent, and God honored his honest questioning.

God has been in control, continues to be in control, and will always be in control. He heard Job each time Job asked for help. He hears us every time we ask for help. We can trust him even when he is silent.

Our lives are not our own. Therefore, we must accept God's will regardless of how it feels. If God is silent, there is a reason. If no signs from heaven are available, know and understand that there is a very good reason for this also.

Kellie Lane

The instructor is always silent when the test is given. ... When God is silent in your life ... you are being tested.

Rick Warren

I believe that God is in me as the sun is in the colour and fragrance of a flower—the Light in my darkness, the Voice in my silence.

Helen Keller

For Further Reflection

Psalm 28:1; Psalm 46:10; Jeremiah 29:11

TODAY'S PRAYER

Merciful Father, I want to be relieved of depression and everything that comes with it. I know that one day I will be healed, but while I am waiting, please be near me in my weakness. Fill me with joy and peace that I know only comes from you. Amen.

Yesterday Instead of Today

Remember not the former things, nor consider the things of old. Behold, I am doing a new thing; now it springs forth, do you not perceive it? I will make a way in the wilderness and rivers in the desert.

Isaiah 43:18–19 ESV

Sometimes we live in the past. The past can be full of joyful memories: the birth of a child or grandchild, a graduation, a wedding, making the sports team. But memories can also bring up sad and difficult times. Thinking about the past is not bad if we use what we learned in those experiences to help us grow. However, when we dwell on the past, we can wallow in negative emotions that leave us unable to enjoy the present.

When we ruminate, we overthink a life event, refusing to let go. We fret about what we could have done differently or fixate on wrongs and injustices. But continuing to rehearse a negative scenario in our minds without any resolution could be contributing to our symptoms of depression.

God knows the suffering and distress we experience in the world (John 16:33). But he wants us to live free of our hurts. He reminds us to bring everything to him and warns us not to take revenge. In fact, he tells us to love our enemies (Luke 6:27–28). This is the part where many of us ask God, "How? Why should I?" God gives us these commands because he knows what hanging on to past hurts can do to our body, mind, and soul. Instead, acknowledge what happened, feel the pain, correct any negative self-talk, and offer the past to

God. When we move out of the past and into the present, we begin to experience a new joy.

Often we look so long at the closed door that we do not see the one that has been opened for us.

Helen Keller

Insisting on living in your past will kill your future. Let it go.

Tony Evans

You can't have a better tomorrow if you're thinking about yesterday.

Charles Kettering

For Further Reflection

Philippians 3:13; 2 Corinthians 5:17; Ephesians 4:31-32

TODAY'S PRAYER

Father, there is so much from my past that I struggle to let go of. When those memories come up, help me to stop replaying them and instead give them to you. Please heal me from my past and lead me on the path to joy. Amen

DAY 32

Today Is Not Tomorrow

Give your entire attention to what God is doing right now, and don't get worked up about what may or may not happen tomorrow. God will help you deal with whatever hard things come up when the time comes.

MATTHEW 6:34 MSG

Unlike some of the best science fiction movies, we can't travel into the future and see how life turns out. We also can't predict a happily-ever-after. We prepare, plan, and work diligently. But there is no guarantee that what we hoped for will ever come to fruition. Some of us are okay with that, knowing that we can do our best, but the future is in God's hands. Others can become so concerned about the future that those worries start to affect us physically, emotionally, and spiritually.

According to the Mayo Clinic, any type of worry or stress that is left unchecked can present as fatigue or trouble sleeping. Our moods can shift between anxiety, irritability, and feeling overwhelmed, all emotions that can potentially lead to social withdrawal, a change in eating habits, or angry outbursts.[6] Sound familiar? Chronic worry can lead to bouts of sadness or depression.

Even though the future is loaded with uncertainty, we do know one thing we can rely on: God shows up repeatedly to provide for his people (Exodus 14–16). We also know that God never changes; he is the same from everlasting to everlasting (Psalm 90:2). The same God in the Bible will show up for us at exactly the right time with exactly what we need. Learning to let go of the things we can't control and leaving them in God's hands takes away the burden. Life is hard. But we don't have to manage it on our own. In his own time, God will bring us to the next step and meet us there with everything we require.

If you must look back, do so forgivingly. If you must look forward, do so prayerfully. However, the wisest thing you can do is to be present in the present. Gratefully.

Maya Angelou

Leave the broken, irreversible past in God's hands, and step out into the invincible future with Him.

Oswald Chambers

For Further Reflection

Psalm 94:19; James 4:13-17; John 14:1

TODAY'S PRAYER

Lord, help me to focus on you and not get so wrapped up in my future that I miss what you are doing today. Please help me to remember you're here with me today and ready to meet me in the future.

Amen

Live for Today

Give us this day, our daily bread.

MATTHEW 6:11 ESV

Sometimes it's easy to focus on everything but the present. We might find ourselves constantly living in a mild state of stress about the future. Will I have enough? Will this circumstance or that trial work out? Or we might be living in regrets of the past, fixating on events that can't be changed. Living in the present is not easy, but Jesus knew that.

In Matthew 6, Jesus taught the disciples to ask God for their "daily bread." Scholars have examined these words, trying to determine what Jesus meant. Some believe Jesus was referring to the food they ate. Others believe Jesus was referring to everything they needed for that day. Either way, these words are a reminder that our thoughts and prayers should be focused first on God, remembering that he is the ultimate Provider, and second, on the certainty that he will give us what is sufficient for "this day." Today is safe in his hands, and we can entrust tomorrow to him as well.

God is asking us to be in the moment. Not distracted by ruminations of the past or worries about the future, but centered on today. In doing so, we have a better chance of managing what is in front of us. As life unfolds, we can respond in a way that is healthy and appropriate, leaving us nothing to regret.

The ability to be in the present moment is a major component of mental wellness.

Abraham Maslow

If you want to be happy, do not dwell in the past, do not worry about the future, focus on living fully in the present.

Roy T. Bennett

Yesterday is gone. Tomorrow has not yet come. We have only today. Let us begin.

Mother Theresa

For Further Reflection

James 4:14; Philippians 4:11; Proverbs 27:1

TODAY'S PRAYER

Lord, I give you today. Please help me quiet my mind and focus on what you have presented in front of me at this time and place. Amen.

Our Battle of Rephidim

Call to Me and I will answer you, and I will tell you
great and mighty things, which you do not know.

Jeremiah 33:3 NASB

Sometimes our battle against depression, whether new or chronic, leaves us worn out. We want to continue in the fight, but no matter what we do, we cannot catch our breath or get relief.

In Exodus 17, the same thing happened to Moses and the Israelites at Rephidim. Moses had just led the Israelites out of Egypt, across the Red Sea. God fought for them and he was the only reason the Egyptians were destroyed. But as the Amalekites approached, God told the Israelites to take up their swords and fight! This did not mean that God stopped fighting for them. In his sovereignty, God might have wanted to teach the Israelites that he would fight through them. The strategy? When Moses prayed with his hands lifted high holding the staff used to part the Red Sea, the Israelites were winning. But Moses became tired and his arms became heavy. When he lowered his arms to rest, the military advantage changed in favor of the Amalekites. When that happened, two of Moses's family members held up his hands for support in prayer.

Have you ever felt like Moses at the battle of Rephidim? There are times when God calls us to fight—and uses other people to support us in the fight. When we are overtaken by the symptoms of depression, we need to rely on God's wisdom that prompts us to call upon our closest friends and family to join us in prayer and to join us in treatment as we march on to conquer our ailments. Those folks will speak for us when we cannot speak. They will help us see when we cannot see clearly. They will hold us up when we are ready to collapse.

God has a plan for our deliverance before our problems ever appear. He is not surprised when trouble comes. He is not in Heaven wringing His hands trying to figure out what to do. He's in control. Our part is to focus on Him and His mighty power, worshipping Him and praising Him for the manifestation of His solution and listening for a word of direction from Him.

Joyce Meyer

There are no words to express the abyss between isolation and having one ally. It may be conceded to the mathematician that four is twice two. But two is not twice one; two is two thousand times one.

G. K. Chesterton

For Further Reflection

Exodus 17; James 1:5; Romans 8:31

TODAY'S PRAYER

Lord, I know all my help comes from you. During this battle, I feel so weary and worn. But help me to remember that you will be my strength, spiritually, emotionally, and physically. Remind me that the battle belongs to you. Amen

Accept Yourself

*And we know that for those who love God
all things work together for good, for those
who are called according to his purpose.*

Romans 8:28 esv

D
epression is more common than we think. Millions of people face varying degrees of depression, but most cases are unreported. Regardless of the severity, we can all relate to the challenges that come with trying to overcome an illness.

The first key is acceptance. Accepting where we are and what we are going through is a step toward healing. Even though we live in a society where open discussion about mental health issues is still taboo, we can make the choice to allow this new dimension to be part of our reality. If we don't, we are bound to continue denying our experience and faking a life that does not exist.

The second key is to let go of blame and labeling ourselves. Sometimes we are the ones who do the greatest damage to ourselves through self-talk. We start to look for ways to explain our circumstances and take the blame for being in the pit. We beat ourselves up by thinking the outcome would have been different if only we had exercised more, forgiven more, been more loving, read more Scripture, or ... fill in the blank.

When we accept and embrace our circumstances, we can begin to allow God's plan to take root. If we treat our illness as the result of our failings, then we are prone to using our own efforts to make ourselves better. If we come to a place of accepting our depression as an event that God allowed, we have access to the full power of God to help us manage and become free from the darkness.

Acceptance of one's life has nothing to do with resignation; it does not mean running away from the struggle. On the contrary, it means accepting it as it comes, with all the handicaps of heredity, of suffering, of psychological complexes and injustices.

Paul Tournier

The worst loneliness is to not be comfortable with yourself.

Mark Twain

"You have peace," the old woman said, "when you make it with yourself."

Mitch Albom

For Further Reflection

Psalm 139:14; Romans 8:1

TODAY'S PRAYER

Creator Father, thank you for making me with such detail. Please help me to accept the circumstances that come my way and bring me to the realization that I am still under your watchful eye. Amen.

Get a Routine

Commit your actions to the LORD,
and your plans will succeed.

PROVERBS 16:3 NLT

The concept of establishing a routine might make some of us cringe, especially those who are less organized. However, we probably already have several routines in our life and don't realize it. Take for example how we put together a meal, how we get to work or school, or how we clean our homes. But for the person experiencing depression, the daily activities of life can look like a mountain that is unpassable.

Depression is a mental suffering that is anti-routine and unpredictable. Managing the basics becomes a chore. Even if we feel we don't have the energy to move, following a schedule is a great way to combat the lethargy. Having a plan can help us manage the symptoms that limit our days.

One of the best ways to combat depression is to begin with a simple routine that starts the minute we open our eyes. It can look like this:

- Take a moment to be grateful. This sets our mind in a direction that recognizes the positive in life.

- Take a minute to stretch—yes, right there in the bed! This can help get the blood flowing and wake up some muscles.

- Move to the shower. Use this time to talk to God. Get a pulse for how you are feeling today and acknowledge it. Set goals for the day.

🌿 Get dressed. Changing clothes is a sure way to trick ourselves into preparing for the day.

These steps might sound simple, but for the person struggling with depressive symptoms, accomplishing these daily practices can be a large task. Do not expect perfection. Start small. Add healthy habits as you go. Be good to yourself.

Small progress is still progress.

Anonymous

You'll never change your life until you change something you do daily.

John C. Maxwell

It was character that got us out of bed, commitment that moved us into action, and discipline that enabled us to follow through.

Zig Ziglar

For Further Reflection

Ecclesiastes 9:10; Proverbs 20:13; Proverbs 24:30–34

TODAY'S PRAYER

Lord, you know each day can be difficult for me. Please meet me where I am and help me to do the next best thing on my journey to health. I know you are with me and will provide strength. Amen.

Renewal

But they who wait for the LORD shall renew their
strength; they shall mount up with wings like eagles;
they shall run and not be weary;
they shall walk and not faint.

ISAIAH 40:31 ESV

Running can feel invigorating. We feel our blood pumping and the strength of our stride. Our senses are receptive to what is happening around us. But long-distance runners will share the other side of the sport. Sometimes their bodies ache or suffer injury. Sometimes they must take a break, giving their bodies a rest. Then when they resume running, they have renewed energy to keep pace.

The trajectory to healing and wholeness can seem long. We might have done everything we know to do—consult with professionals, partner with others who have run this race—yet we hit a wall and feel as if we cannot go any further. Our pace slows from a run to a walk. Our breaks become longer until eventually we consider staying on the sidelines. But we are not done yet.

Scripture talks a great deal about relying on God to do what seems impossible. Reaching our goal of better health requires that same reliance. If we choose to wait for him, we will receive renewed energy from the Lord. We might find a new treatment. We might see improvement due to consistency in following professional advice. A friend might offer a kind word that helps us refocus and get back into the race. We get on the path at a slower pace and eventually build up our stride. Before we know it, we are running our race as if we were being carried by eagles' wings.

If you are renewed by grace, and were to meet your old self, I am sure you would be very anxious to get out of his company.

Charles Spurgeon

To be fully alive, you need time with God to recharge.

Craig Groeschel

When you take time with God and listen to his voice, he renews your strength and enables you to handle life.

Joyce Meyer

For Further Reflection

Psalm 31:4; Psalm 18:32; Isaiah 40:29

TODAY'S PRAYER

God, thank you for the reminder that in you I have the strength I need on this path. Please help me to remember that I can bring my weariness to you. Please forgive me for trying to do this in my own power. Amen.

Illness, the Thief

The thief comes only to steal and kill and destroy.
I came that they may have life and have it abundantly.

JOHN 10:10 ESV

We all have times in our lives when we decide to purge. We find things we have not used in years and decide to bag them up and donate them to charity so someone else can use them. Choosing to give something away is vastly different from having something taken away, especially something like our health.

We might do everything right regarding our health. We eat right, exercise, and keep up with doctor appointments, but one day something shifts. Our zeal for life and activities disappears. We are visited by an intruder—depression. It is faceless, silent, and can be lethal. This thief leaves us numb. It steals our time, our hope, our joy.

When we have been robbed of our health, we can find peace in knowing we still have one sure thing that cannot be taken from us, and that is God. John 10:10 tells us that God knows about the "thieves" that come into our lives, and he promises to give us a life that is more abundant, more than plentiful, and more than bountiful.

We might feel robbed of how things used to be. But God can restore things to even better than they used to be, whether that happen here on earth or one day in glory when, as Romans 8:23 reminds us, we will receive the full redemption of our bodies. Meanwhile, we can rest in the certainty that we belong to God. We have eternal life. And that is something no thief can steal.

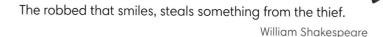

The robbed that smiles, steals something from the thief.

William Shakespeare

Mental illness is a thief that can rob you of your purpose, goals, sense of identity, and belief that you have anything significant to offer the world. You may feel like you are always a burden and never a blessing, but God says you are needed! What you've gone through can be a source of hope and healing to others.

Kay Warren

I can't change the direction of the wind, but I can adjust my sails to always reach my destination.

Jimmy Dean

For Further Reflection

James 5:15; Psalm 103:2-3; Psalm 130:5

TODAY'S PRAYER

God, thank you for the promise of your power to restore what depression has taken from me. Please help me to let go of what I think is good in my life and surrender to your definition of the best. Give me wisdom and endurance as I follow you. Amen.

No Separation

For I am sure that neither death nor life, nor angels
nor rulers, nor things present nor things to come,
nor powers, nor height nor depth, nor anything else
in all creation, will be able to separate us from
the love of God in Christ Jesus our Lord.

Romans 8:38–39 esv

Sometimes when we sense the presence of God, it leaves us speechless. We might feel his presence on a quiet walk in nature or after we have spent our one-on-one time with him. Sometimes we feel his presence during a worship gathering. Such closeness is like no other feeling. The holy God, who sits high on his throne, makes his presence known to us—sinners who can so easily neglect our relationship with him. Yet, day after day, his presence is there when we seek him.

Even when we do our part to connect with him, sometimes we feel separated from the Lord. How can that be? We've spent time with him. We've experienced a peace or joy that we cannot explain, but then something happens that leaves us feeling alone. A death. A job loss. A regret. An illness. We can feel as though we are behind a wall with no doors or windows. We cry out and hear no response. We think we are alone.

When we are distracted by the darkness of whatever we are going through, it can be easy to forget what Scripture says. Today's passage tells us that nothing separates us from his love. He is there for us. He is aware of what is occurring and even though we may not see it or feel it, he is already working out his plan concerning us. We must call out to God, in faith, trusting he is still there, and he hears us.

Two prisoners whose cells adjoin communicate with each other by knocking on the wall. The wall is the thing which separates them but is also their means of communication. It is the same with us and God. Every separation is a link.

Simone Weil

When you are wired to God in a unique way, nothing can separate you from the love of God.

T. B. Joshua

Nothing can separate you from God's love, absolutely nothing. God is enough for time, God is enough for eternity. God is enough!

Hannah Whitall Smith

For Further Reflection

Romans 8:31; 2 Timothy 4:17; John 3:16

TODAY'S PRAYER

Father, there are times when I cannot feel your presence. In those times, I am likely to forget your promise of always being with me. Please help me remember that even in my darkest times, you are right by my side. Amen.

Due Diligence

More than anything you guard, protect your mind,
for life flows from it.

PROVERBS 4:23 CEB

When we decide to work toward a goal, we spend a great deal of time preparing. We research. Find the right tools. Develop a plan that we believe will help us achieve that goal. If we consider the time we spent—from conceptualization to completion—we might be surprised to see we invested more time preparing than actually working toward the goal. That's because when we set out to do something, we need the right resources to reach our goal.

The same applies to our goal of improving our mental health. When we start to experience depressive symptoms, it can be easy to reach for the easiest thing to provide relief. We skim the latest article addressing our issue. We try doing what we heard someone else did. But a quick fix is just that—short-term relief. Aside from emergency medicine administered by a qualified professional, a quick fix is not beneficial in the long-term.

It is important to do some work to find the most qualified professional available to us. If possible, we should try to find a professional who knows Jesus Christ and believes in his healing power. Whether we're researching a recovery group or a professional counselor, we want to know: Are they safe? Is there grace and acceptance? Is the Bible the source of recovery or an add-on?

Trusting our mental health to the latest fad might bring quick respite, but complete restoration of body, mind, and soul needs to be in the care of trained layperson or professional. Taking the time to investigate is vital, because the long-term effects of choosing the wrong healing path can add more pain than relief.

Give me six hours to chop down a tree and I will spend the first four sharpening the ax.

Abraham Lincoln

An ounce of prevention is worth a pound of cure.

Benjamin Franklin

If you're proactive, you focus on preparing. If you're reactive, you end up focusing on repairing.

John C. Maxwell

For Further Reflection

2 Peter 1:5; Proverbs 10:4; Proverbs 12:27

TODAY'S PRAYER

Father, I am to the point where I need help from others. Forgive me for the times when I took a shortcut to get to the end more quickly. Give me wisdom as I find the right help. Amen.

Choose Your Friends Wisely

He who walks [as a companion] with wise men will be wise, But the companions of [conceited, dull-witted] fools [are fools themselves and] will experience harm.

PROVERBS 13:20 AMP

Relationships are the backbone of life. We have acquaintances, besties, husbands or wives. It is impossible to live a healthy lifestyle without relationships, and research shows that friends are important to our psychological well-being.

Because the people in our lives play such a huge role on our mental health, we should pay attention to those we let into our lives and how much access we give them. Good friends are good for the soul! They will celebrate in the good times and be with us in the bad times.

So how do we pick the "right" people, those who will not leave us stranded on our worst days? There is no simple answer, but we can look for the following traits:

- *Integrity.* Are they trustworthy and dependable, or will they leave when life becomes challenging?

- *Care.* Do they show empathy when we share about a difficult day? Can they hear and listen to what we have to say? Can they sit in silence with us?

We might struggle to reach out to others, especially in the midst of our depressive symptoms. And sometimes in our loneliness we accept anyone's behavior as a sign that they care about us. However, not everyone is equipped to walk with us in every season. We need to be intentional about the people we allow to be our supporters. Regardless of our circumstances, it is never too late to make good friends.

When we honestly ask ourselves which person in our lives means the most to us, we often find that it is those who, instead of giving advice, solutions, or cures, have chosen rather to share our pain and touch our wounds with a warm and tender hand.

Henri Nouwen

I would rather walk with a friend in the dark, than alone in the light.

Helen Keller

Friends are those rare people who ask how we are and then wait to hear the answer.

Ed Cunningham

For Further Reflection

1 Thessalonians 5:11; Ecclesiastes 4:9; Proverbs 18:24

TODAY'S PRAYER

Dear Jesus, you are a friend who sticks close to me always. Please help me as I choose my support team, that they will carry Christlike attributes. Amen.

Laugh a Little

Then young women will dance and be glad, young men and old as well. I will turn their mourning into gladness; I will give them comfort and joy instead of sorrow.

JEREMIAH 31:13

Children laugh the best. They laugh often, not only with their faces but also with their whole bodies. Laughter is the one language that looks and sounds the same everywhere. Laughter makes us feel good. We might think the effects are momentary, but according to science, the effects of laughter can last all day as we think back to what made us laugh.

When life gets serious, we forget to laugh. Although laughter cannot cure sickness, research increasingly indicates that laughter is good for our bodies.

- Laughter decreases stress hormones and improves our immunity to infection.
- Laughter triggers the release of feel-good chemicals.
- Laughter (or a simple smile) can help us cope with difficult situations.
- Laughter can bring people together.

You can't focus on negative emotions at the same time you're laughing.

When we are in the depths of a challenge, laughter is likely the last thing on our minds. And there is nothing funny about the circumstances we are experiencing. However, laughter has incredible power to bring relief and renewal.

Laughter is a resource that is fun, free, and easy. So find a safe person, watch an old comedy variety show, test your knowledge of knock-knock jokes, maybe play a fun, interactive game, and see if your mood doesn't lift.

Humor is a prelude to faith and laughter is the beginning of prayer.

Reinhold Niebuhr

Laugh till you weep. Weep till there's nothing left but to laugh at your weeping. In the end it's all one.

Frederick Buechner

Laughter is the closest thing to the grace of God.

Karl Barth

For Further Reflection

Proverbs 17:22; Psalm126:2; Job 8:21; Proverbs 15:13

TODAY'S PRAYER

Jesus, laughing is so not on my radar right now. But I ask you to show me things that can bring a smile to my face and a chuckle to my belly. Amen.

The Great Physician

He heals the brokenhearted and binds up their wounds.

PSALM 147:3 ESV

Many people in the Bible who had an encounter with Jesus received physical healing: the man with leprosy; Peter's mother-in-law; the paralyzed man; the man with the withered hand; the woman with an issue of blood; the blind, deaf, mute and those overtaken by evil spirits and demons. In an instant, Jesus proclaimed healing and it was so. But what about the wounds of today?

Hebrews 13:8 tells us Jesus is the same yesterday, today, and forever. The Lord who healed all those people in the Bible thousands of years ago is the same one who can heal us today. We all have witnessed or heard of physical healings that can occur—healings from cancer, the flu, broken bones. Healing might come from natural remedies or medicine, or a combination of both. But as Christians, we know that, ultimately, healing is in God's hands.

Emotional healing might be more difficult to "see." Emotional wounds can be more painful than physical injuries. No medicine can touch the pain of an absent parent, rejection, betrayal, or losing a loved one. But Jesus can heal those types of wounds also. He is the only one who can heal and restore our emotional well-being. Medical professionals can relieve suffering and save lives. But our faith should not rest solely in physicians. Our faith needs to be in God.

Christ is the most cheap physician, he takes no fee. He desires us to bring nothing to him but broken hearts; and when he has cured us he desires us to bestow nothing on him but our love.

Thomas Watson

There is not a formula for the way that God heals. There's not a timetable.

Amy Grant

For Further Reflection

Mark 2:17; Jeremiah 17:14; Jeremiah 30:17; Hosea 6:1

TODAY'S PRAYER

God, forgive me for coming to you only when I have exhausted all my resources. Please give me peace in the situation I am facing. And please give me the spiritual healing you see fit. Amen.

Weighed Down

Let us throw off everything that hinders and the sin that so easily entangles. And let us run with perseverance the race marked out for us, fixing our eyes on Jesus, the pioneer and perfecter of faith.

HEBREWS 12:1–2

People remember the sinking of the RMS Titanic as one of the greatest maritime tragedies of all time. The British ship was thought to meet the highest standard in accommodations, technology, power, and safety. Some of the world's most prominent people of that time purchased a ticket, traveling first class. At the time of its construction, the Titanic was the largest cruise ship of its kind and was thought to be unsinkable. On April 14, 1912, the ship hit an iceberg, and the impact bent the hull inward, exposing the seams. Water seeped in, weighing down the ship, and caused it to sink and many lives to be lost.

The Christian life can also be weighed down by disappointment, loss, or anguish, causing us to lose hope for our future and sink into despair. For those suffering depression, that weight might have us in dry dock, watching others launch into life. What keeps us weighed down? Is it physical, a chemical imbalance, unforgiveness, bitterness, or something else? Similar to the extravagantly decorated Titanic, we might project a well-decorated appearance. But if our bodies or souls have been breached by external forces, and we aren't leaning hard into God's strength and grace, negative thoughts, behaviors, and emotions can threaten to drown us. The writer of Hebrews encourages us to examine our lives and remove anything that impedes our progress.

Unlike the Titanic's unhappy outcome, when our ship is battered by trials and hardships and when we find our progress slowing—or stopping—we can surrender everything to Jesus Christ and, with his strength and surety, keep sailing ahead.

For you to rise up, you need to give up on that which is constantly pulling you down.

Gift Gugu Mona

The greatest glory in living lies not in never falling, but in rising every time we fall.

Nelson Mandela

Keep on going, and the chances are that you will stumble on something, perhaps when you are least expecting it. I never heard of anyone ever stumbling on something sitting down.

Charles F. Kettering

For Further Reflection

Matthew 11:28-30; Acts 20:24

TODAY'S PRAYER

Lord, thank you for helping me make it this far. Help me see where I am weighed down and be willing to let it go. Thank you that I can press in close to you today. Amen.

A Secret Weapon

Is anyone among you suffering? Let him pray.
Is anyone cheerful? Let him sing praise.

JAMES 5:13 ESV

In the book of 2 Chronicles we read that Israel was split between the northern kingdom and the southern kingdom. In chapter 20, a couple of the neighboring nations decide they are going to attack Judah, the southern kingdom. Judah's king, Jehoshaphat, fasts and prays, and he receives prophecy that Judah will win without a fight. On the day of battle, Jehoshaphat still prepares and sends out his best singers who lead the way, praising God. With Judah's secret weapon—songs of praise—the attacking nations become confused, attack each other, and end their own lives.

Can you imagine?

Soldier: "What's the plan, General?"

General: "We are going to send out the singers."

To our thinking, this is probably the most illogical plan of attack. When faced with a challenge, singing songs of praise—worshiping God—is often the last thing we want to do. Instead, we focus on the problem. We try to overcome the obstacle in our own strength and understanding, which only saps our energy. But when we turn our focus to God and worship him, our battle is assuredly won. The act of worshiping releases the power of God as we proclaim his strength.

When we worship, God works. We become refreshed; we find peace and a sense of joy. We can dare to look our enemy in the eye and shout as David did against Goliath, "You come against me with sword and spear and javelin, but I come against you in the name of the Lord Almighty, the God of the armies of Israel" (1 Samuel 17:45).

In worship, we discover the breathtaking strength of God as we witness him fight for us.

If you don't worship … you'll never experience God.

David Jeremiah

The heart of God loves a persevering worshipper who, though overwhelmed by many troubles, is overwhelmed even more by the beauty of God.

Matt Redman

Without worship, we go about miserable.

A. W. Tozer

For Further Reflection

2 Chronicles 20:20-22; Hebrews 13:15; Psalm 150:2

TODAY'S PRAYER

Lord, I chose to praise and worship you in the middle of my circumstances. I chose to bless you when my spirit is weak. You alone will have the glory and the victory. Amen.

Pain Does Have a Purpose

Consider it pure joy, my brothers and sisters, whenever you face trials of many kinds, because you know that the testing of your faith produces perseverance. Let perseverance finish its work so that you may be mature and complete, not lacking anything.

JAMES 1:2–4

Trials and suffering can make us frustrated, irritable, and angry. Maybe it is an ongoing riff in the family. Maybe it is a job where we feel drained and morale is low. Maybe it is an illness that worsens over time despite our best efforts to get better. God seems silent. Prayers are not answered the way we would like.

But what if God allows the pain in our lives for a reason?

Sometimes God uses pain to refine us. One of the best ways to shape character is through adversity. Through trials, we can learn humility, trust, and faith. We gain a clearer picture of who we are, including our tendency toward pridefulness and self-sufficiency. As God walks with us through the trials, he refines us to be more like Christ. God can provide opportunities for us to use the insight we gain from our trials to minister to others. Second Corinthians 1:3–4 says that God "comforts us in all our troubles, so that we can comfort those in any trouble with the comfort we ourselves receive from God." We can use our difficult experiences to walk with someone else who's experiencing a similar trial. God could also be preparing us for work that we're not ready for yet. God knows exactly what to include in our lives to help us build endurance, strength, and faith so that we are prepared for the task he has ahead. Our experiences can help us minister God's love and share eternal hope with others.

Nothing we go through is arbitrary. In the midst of our trials, we can look for opportunities God might give us—both now and in the days ahead—to grow in our walk with him and to be an encouragement to those around us.

No pain, no palm; no thorns, no throne; no gall, no glory; no cross, no crown.

William Penn

God never allows pain without a purpose.

Jerry Bridges

Your greatest ministry will most likely come out of your greatest hurt.

Rick Warren

For Further Reflection

1 Peter 1:6–7; Isaiah 48:10; 1 Corinthians 13:12

TODAY'S PRAYER

God, I admit I do not like the idea that you allow pain as a way to refine me or bless others. I also do not understand why you allow this pain to happen. But I can trust your character and your history, knowing that you see the big picture. Amen.

The Squeaky Wheel

*So I say to you, ask and keep on asking, and it will
be given to you; seek and keep on seeking, and
you will find; knock and keep on knocking,
and the door will be opened to you.*

LUKE 11:9 AMP

"The squeaky wheel gets the grease" is a popular American proverb used to convey that the loudest, most noticeable issue is the one that will get attention. When something is off in our body, mind, or spirit, that issue might become a squeaky wheel that we are quick to notice. We promptly search for an answer, reach out to professionals, or follow trusted advice and hopefully experience relief. But maybe we search for the cause, visit numerous medical professionals, and yet find no answers or relief. The repeated but futile searching might tempt us to give up.

However, the Bible encourages us to persevere. In Luke 18, a widow pleads with a judge to right a wrong done to her. She approaches him repeatedly, and he eventually caves and avenges the wrong done against her. In the story, she could be seen as the squeaky wheel who persisted until she got some type of resolution. Luke explains in verse 1 that the purpose of the parable was to teach us to always pray and never give up.

Being on the journey to find relief from depression can be frustrating. But trust that God hears and is working in his time to heal. Continue to seek God and his direction for healing. God will not be offended by our repeated requests.

He is our loving Father who cares about us. He hears us every time we bring a concern to him. We might feel as though we're a squeaky wheel, but the Lord welcomes our prayers and encourages us to approach him anytime.

Never, never, never, never give up.

Winston Churchill

Never give up, for that is just the place and time that the tide will turn.

Harriet Beecher Stowe

Some people think God does not like to be troubled with our constant coming and asking. The way to trouble God is not to come at all.

D. L. Moody

For Further Reflection

1 John 5:14-15; Isaiah 55:8-9; Matthew 7:7-11

TODAY'S PRAYER

Lord, I feel like a broken record but I come to you again and ask for relief from this depression. I ask for guidance to find the right professionals and resources. Thank you that I can keep calling on you, knowing that you hear and care. Amen.

The Challenge of Change

Don't copy the behavior and customs of this world, but let God transform you into a new person by changing the way you think. Then you will learn to know God's will for you, which is good and pleasing and perfect.

ROMANS 12:2 NLT

Change is inevitable. Whether it be a small adjustment or a major shift in our life, change can be exciting as we face new experiences, new people, and new places. However, some transitions are not so exciting. Maybe the change we're facing is the result of a supervisor's decision to give us more work and less hours. Maybe our children are becoming young adults and we have to transition to life with an empty nest. Maybe we're facing an unwanted change in a personal relationship.

What can we do to help manage the emotional waves that come with change? We can remember that God is with us. After forty years of wilderness wandering, God's people were preparing to enter the promised land. Moses had died, and Joshua was in charge. God told Joshua to "be strong and very courageous. Be careful to obey all the laws my servant Moses gave you; do not turn from it to the right or to the left, that you may be successful wherever you go" (Joshua 1:7). God's laws and his promise of continued faithfulness provided the stability needed during this pivotal period of transition, both for the Israelites and for Joshua as their new leader.

Second, during periods of change, we need to keep God at the center of our focus. In Matthew 19:21 Jesus instructed the rich young ruler to sell all his possessions and follow him. But Scripture states that the young man "went away sad" (Matthew 19:22). He missed what Jesus was offering because he valued his wealth and property more.

Because we know that God is with us at all times, we should strive to see beyond the change in our circumstances and look at the opportunity he is providing to develop and grow.

Change always starts in your mind. The way you think determines the way you feel, and the way you feel influences the way you act.

Rick Warren

Will power does not change men. Time does not change men. Christ does.

Henry Drummond

Concentrate on counting your blessings and you'll have little time to count anything else.

Woodrow Kroll

For Further Reflection

Ecclesiastes 3:1-8; Proverbs 16:3; Joshua 1:6-11

TODAY'S PRAYER

Lord, I am uncomfortable and unclear about where life is taking me right now. But I know as long as I remember you are with me and keep my focus on you, I can navigate this change with your grace and mercy. Amen.

God, Don't You Care?

*O LORD, how long shall I cry for help,
and you will not hear?*

HABAKKUK 1:2 ESV

Some of us have this same question in our hearts that the prophet Habakkuk asked—but we dare not ask it. The question seems so disrespectful. But the Bible gives us two instances where people asked Jesus the same question. The first takes place with the disciples in the boat as they are crossing a lake. A storm approaches and tosses the boat, the waves crashing with enough force to destroy it. The second occurs at a dinner party hosted by Mary and Martha. As Martha is preparing the meal in the kitchen, she becomes irritated that Mary isn't helping. In both stories, the question is asked, "Lord, don't you care?"

We can probably all relate to times like these when we feel overwhelmed and alone. So how should we manage a situation when it seems our prayers go unanswered or God hasn't stepped in and fixed everything? First, we should be honest with God about how we are feeling. We can voice our perceptions and expectations without fear of reprisal. Second, we can trust God's history. If we look back over our lives, we can see how God has provided for us, even when we didn't ask. Third, we can remember that God's care for us does not mean the circumstances will always resolve as we expect. Sometimes God resolves our problems exactly as we have asked. Other times, we experience many twists and turns before he brings the resolution he sees fit.

We have to be intentional about letting go of our demands on God. We have to surrender and sit at his feet and learn from him as we persevere.

God is just as merciful in the things he does not allow, as he is in the things he does.

Andrena Sawyer

The Bible tells us that God will meet all our needs. He feeds the birds of the air and clothes the grass with the splendor of lilies. How much more, then, will he care for us, who are made in his image?

Charles Stanley

God sometimes answers our prayers by giving us what we would have asked for had we known what he knows.

J. D. Greear

For Further Reflection

Mark 4:35–40; Luke 10:38–42; Habakkuk 1:1–11; Psalm 77:1–20

TODAY'S PRAYER

I confess my doubts. So often I want life to go the way I think is best. Help me to trust you in all circumstances, knowing that you are working out your purposes in my life. Amen.

Identity in Christ

*But to all who did receive him, who believed in his name,
he gave the right to become children of God.*

JOHN 1:12 ESV

We live in a world where our identity is often formed by what we do (our job, our hobbies, the role we play at work or at church, grades in school, etc.). We experience pressures to perform and can often think that how we perform determines our worth. When we can't perform as we'd like—or as other people might expect us to—our view of ourselves can be shaken, leaving us to search for a way to reinvent or redefine ourselves.

When we face what appears to be a failure in the world's eyes, or an unexpected diagnosis that reshapes how we see ourselves, we have to recognize the false thinking and replace it with the truths of Scripture.

We must recognize that if we've placed our trust in Jesus, we are God's child—"fearfully and wonderfully made" (Psalm 139:14) and loved deeply by him. We can use a diagnosis to help describe what we are feeling—not define who we are. The label of the diagnosis reduces our complexity to commonness. And because scripture says we are each uniquely made, we are anything but common (Matthew 10:30; Genesis 1:27).

When our identity is rooted in Christ, we believe that what God says about us is truer than what anyone else says—including ourselves. So yes, find a qualified professional to provide an appropriate diagnosis, but remember it is only a description of your experience; it doesn't define you.

Jesus came to announce to us that an identity based on success, popularity and power is a false identity—an illusion! Loudly and clearly he says: "You are not what the world makes you; but you are children of God."

Henri Nouwen

The more we focus on who we are in Christ, the less it matters who we were in the past, or even what happened to us.

Joyce Meyer

You discover your identity and purpose through a relationship with Jesus Christ.

Rick Warren

For Further Reflection

Ephesians 2:10; Galatians 2:20; 1 Peter 2:9; Psalm 139

TODAY'S PRAYER

Lord, I pray that you will reveal any areas in my life in which I'm failing to find my identity in you. Teach me to hear what you say about me over the distractions and lies of the world. Amen.

When Things Don't Go Well

*We know that all things work together for good for those
who love God, who are called according to his purpose.*

ROMANS 8:28 NRSV

We are creatures of comfort. Given the option, we
will choose the path that gets us where we want
to go with the least disruption and in the least
time. But as we all know, life seldom goes as planned. And
when it doesn't, the first words that many people quote are
from Romans 8:28. But those are not the words most people
want to hear. It's hard to believe that something good can
and will come out of what we believe to be our darkest hour.

However, many events in Scripture show God's sovereignty
over all aspects of life, and his power to bring good from a
bad situation. One such story is that of Joseph, who was sold
into slavery by his brothers. They were jealous of Joseph
and wanted him gone. Joseph endured years of uncertainty
and doubt about his future. As the story unfolds, we can
see the larger picture behind the twenty-three years Joseph
endured slavery, imprisonment, and trials. We learn that
because of Joseph's faithfulness, even in prison, he was
promoted to a position of power in Egypt that provided him
the opportunity to save his family—and his nation—from a
severe famine. In God's sovereignty, Joseph was in Egypt
at the right time. As he told his brothers in Genesis 50:20,
"You intended to harm me, but God intended it for good to
accomplish what is now being done, the saving of many lives.

When our lives are turned upside down, it is hard to understand how anything good can result. In fact, we might not gain full understanding this side of heaven. But in our trial, we can trust that God's plan for those who are called by him includes a greater purpose, even if we can't see it right now.

The idea of redemption is always good news, even if it means sacrifice or some difficult times.

Patti Smith

Keep calm when things don't go according to your expectations. Beautiful things always meet friction.

Ernest Agyemang Yeboah

When things do not go your way, remember that every challenge—every adversity—contains within it seeds of opportunity and growth.

Roy T. Bennett

For Further Reflection

Job 42:1-2; Psalm 40:5; Romans 11:33

TODAY'S PRAYER

Lord, I don't understand why you chose me to have this illness. I confess I struggle to see what good can be in this. But I trust that, in your hands, this journey will give you the glory. Amen.

The Gift of Tears

Jesus wept.

JOHN 11:35

Tears are a part of life. Crying is an emotional response to something we feel. Sometimes we cry in response to something of beauty. We cry at the movies or reading a story. We cry at life events such as the birth of a baby, a graduation, or a memorial service. We cry in anger or confusion.

Tears provide an outlet for our deepest emotions. When we cry, we are vulnerable and authentic. Crying is a letting down of the guard, ultimately a release that cannot be explained in words. Sometimes we fight that vulnerability. Sometimes we believe we shouldn't feel a particular way or we can't identify the cause for the tears. But we can be comforted in knowing that God hears our cries and sees every tear we shed.

Our ability to express our emotions with tears is a gift, and we are in good company because Jesus expressed his emotions through tears. We should not be ashamed of the gift God created in us. When we cry, it should bring us to our heavenly Father so he can remind us that he is with us and loves us. He knows our pain. Scriptures says that he is "close to the brokenhearted and saves those who are crushed in spirit" (Psalm 34:18).

Then God takes it a step further. John 16:20 says, "But your grief will turn to joy." Such transformation can only be orchestrated by God. It's an amazing gift that emotions of both sorrow and joy can bring relief from our greatest pain.

The tears are the blood of the Soul.

Augustine of Hippo

We need never be ashamed of our tears.

Charles Dickens

Tears are God's gift to us. Our holy water. They heal us as they flow.

Rita Schiano

For Further Reflection

Romans 12:15; Psalm 30:5; Psalm 56:8; Revelation 7:17

TODAY'S PRAYER

Lord, I thank you for the gift of tears. Please help me to remember that you accept them as an offering in release of my circumstances. Amen.

The Size of God

Now to him who is able to [carry out his purpose and] do
superabundantly more than all that we dare ask or think
[infinitely beyond our greatest prayers, hopes, or dreams],
according to his power that is at work within us.

EPHESIANS 3:20 AMP

The tallest trees are the California redwoods which can grow more than 350 feet tall, reach a diameter of 24 feet, and weigh as much as 1.6 million pounds.[7] In photographs, people standing at the base of redwoods look miniscule, the size of ants next to a human.

Now think about the God who created those giant redwoods. He created the vastness of the universe, including the parts we cannot see or have not discovered. He is everywhere. He stands outside time, not limited by that construct. He commands the breeze, instructs the oceans to stop on land, and orchestrates the thunderstorms. He existed before everything. With a word, he brought the universe into being, and by his great power all things hold together. We can never see the height or breadth of God and his power.

Compared to his infiniteness, everything else is miniscule. When we contemplate his might and majesty, our lives might seem inconsequential. However, the Bible tells us that the God of all creation cares about us and knows everything we go though. As the storms of life—whether they be financial crisis, homelessness, or illness—threaten to overwhelm, we can remind ourselves that our God is bigger than whatever challenges or heartaches we face. He has no obstacles. Our problem might seem insurmountable. But when we lay it at the foot of Jesus, he towers over all of it.

Don't focus on the size of your problem. Focus on the size of your God.

Tony Evans

How big is your God? The size of your God determines the size of everything.

Howard G. Hendricks

If your problem is too big for you, it's just the right size for God.

Steven Furtick

For Further Reflection

Exodus 15:11; Isaiah 40:22; Ephesians 1:19; Jeremiah 32:27

TODAY'S PRAYER

Thank you for the reminder that you are bigger than my mind can comprehend. Thank you that I can bring my pain and troubles to you, knowing that you can and will address them in your power. Amen.

The Secret of God

The secret things belong to the LORD our God,
but the things which are revealed and disclosed
belong to us and to our children forever, so that
we may do all of the words of this law.

DEUTERONOMY 29:29 AMP

God is all knowing, ever present, all powerful, and the creator of everything. We are limited and finite. We could spend our lives dedicated to learning and yet never attain full knowledge. God has given us the Bible and chosen to share some of his mysteries with us. But parts of the Bible we will never fully understand. In fact, some things we could never understand because they are simply hidden from us. We cannot comprehend the mind of God.

Have you ever asked God why something happened? Why this timing? Why this job loss? Why this illness? In our limited knowledge, no answer seems good enough to justify our suffering. God is the only one who knows the beginning from the end. He is the only one who can answer our *why*. Most times, he chooses not to provide the answer immediately. Instead, he walks with us through the trial, teaching us to lean on him and build our faith.

Although the reason why God allows discomfort into our lives might remain a secret, we can trust he is in full control. Philippians 1:6 promises that we can be "confident of this, that he who began a good work in you will carry it on to completion until the day of Christ Jesus."

When we enter a season of difficulty and the purpose remains a mystery, instead of asking "Why me?" we can try asking "Why not me?"—and then be patient, watching as his plan unfolds in our lives.

It is important for God to arrange our circumstances in such a way that we eventually have to face ourselves.

Joyce Meyer

I would rather walk every day in the darkness with a God who remains a mystery to me than in the light with a God I completely understand.

Kay Warren

The mystery of God hugs you in its all-encompassing arm.

Hildegard of Bingen

For Further Reflection

Psalm 25:14; Jeremiah 33:3; Daniel 2:22

TODAY'S PRAYER

God, I don't pretend to understand why my life has unfolded the way it has. But I can begin to understand that under your vision, nothing is by accident. Please help me to rely on your knowledge, not my own. Amen

Timing Is Everything

*For there is a proper time and procedure for every
matter, though a person may be weighed down by misery.*

ECCLESIASTES 8:6

We all want good things for our lives. But because we live in a fallen world, life is full of what we could interpret as interruptions or detours on our path. As we deal with the unexpected, we must look to God to guide us in the next step or toward the next milestone. Our normal instinct is to want deliverance from whatever has derailed us from our plan. We can be tempted to ask, "When God?" If we have been waiting for something for a while, or if a prayer isn't answered the way we think it should be, it can start to feel as though God didn't hear our prayer or doesn't want to answer even though he could. How do we wait for an answer—his answer—and submit to his timing without becoming bitter?

There is no easy answer, but the Bible provides numerous examples of men and women (Abraham, Jacob, David, and Hannah, to name a few) who had to wait for God to answer. As they waited, they probably felt confused by his silence, wondering what they should do next. But their examples of patience and perseverance show us that waiting is part of what it means to walk in faith. God has us on a trajectory toward what is good. He sees the whole picture and he also knows that, quite often, our solutions to the issues will not take us where he wants to get us. We want the fix now, but his timing is perfect, even though the answer might seem delayed to us.

God's answers happen at exactly the right time! God is working out his master plan. We can trust that when he has us wait, it is for a good purpose.

We must learn to move according to the timetable of the Timeless One and be at peace.

Elisabeth Elliot

Everything is subject to God's timing and everything depends on it.

Sunday Adelaja

Sometimes when we say "God is silent," what's really going on is that he hasn't told the story the way we wanted it told. He will be silent when we want him to fill in the blanks of the story we are creating. But with his own stories, the ones we live in, he is seldom silent.

Paul E. Miller

For Further Reflection

Psalm 31:15; Habakkuk 2:3; Galatians 6:9

TODAY'S PRAYER

Lord, I know I grow impatient while waiting for you to answer my prayer. Thank you that you are coordinating things I do not know about and working the details for a purpose that glorifies your name. Amen.

Say Yes

*For no matter how many promises God has made,
they are "Yes" in Christ. And so through him
the "Amen" is spoken by us to the glory of God.*

2 Corinthians 1:20

The Christian life is about surrendering to the call and will of God. If God is who he says, and if he can do what he says he can, agreeing to whatever he brings into our lives seems like a logical course of action. We're agreeing to a life led by God. We're agreeing to whatever he has planned and whatever challenges he already knows we will encounter.

But the challenges that enter our lives might cause us to second-guess our yes. Maybe we believed that only good things would come our way. Maybe we're realizing that saying yes to God can be scary. It can be overwhelming. But it can also be exciting!

The Bible is full of stories of people who said yes to God without fully knowing what they were signing up for. David was the youngest of his family and worked in the fields. But God called David to be king. As amazing and incredible as that might sound, the reality is he spent years living in caves and on the run on the way to the throne, often in fear for his life. Probably not what he would have signed up for. What about Paul? Paul had a reputation for persecuting Christians, and then God called him to be one of them. Pretty sure Paul did not see that coming. Both people surrendered to the will of God even when it wasn't easy, and the outcome was better than they could have imagined.

Saying yes to God does not mean life will be easy. In that *yes*, we are signing up to be an instrument in God's grand plan. We are signing up to leave our comfort zones and take risks, knowing that God is writing the story with a better ending than even we would write for ourselves.

Outside our comfort zone, though, is where we experience the true awesomeness of God.

Lysa TerKeurst

I am Thy servant to do Thy will, and that will is sweeter to me than position or riches or fame, and I choose it above all things on Earth or in Heaven.

A. W. Tozer

Destiny waits in the hand of God, shaping the still unshapen.

T. S. Eliot

For Further Reflection

1 Corinthians 15:58; 1 Samuel 3:10; Ephesians 6:14

TODAY'S PRAYER

Father, please forgive me for saying no to you.
Thank you for the reassurance that in surrendering
to you, my life is part of your design. When you ask
something of me, help me say yes. Amen.

Lean on Him

For I, the LORD your God, hold your right hand; it is I who say to you, "Fear not, I am the one who helps you."

ISAIAH 41:13 ESV

When we have reached the point of desperation, how do we respond? Our hearts might start to race. Our thoughts escape. We feel confused, scared, and just want relief. We can be tempted to ignore everything we know about God's Word and God's proven history of always being with us.

In moments such as these, we are called to rely on God and have faith that he is our sufficiency. In fact, it's good to constantly remind ourselves that we are totally dependent on God for all our moments.

Why is being mindful of God's sufficiency so vital? First, God is the one who meets our daily needs, and we sometimes have a tendency to forget that. Second, we will reach a point (if we haven't already) when we realize we don't have what we need—and we have no way to attain it in our own strength. If we have not developed the habit of trusting that God provides for us and meets us where we are, we will not suddenly remember the calm assurance that God is the source of our strength, that he is our everything, in moments of desperation.

God doesn't reveal his full plan to us. If he did, we would be prone to avoid it. We might start to manipulate situations to circumvent the difficult times. We might be tempted to try to take control of our destinies, relying on ourselves so that we never have to depend on anyone else.

God only gives us today. Not even that—he gives us this moment. And whether the moment we're in is good or bad, we are depending on God. The same God who allows the blessings also allows the blessings in disguise. And this same God is holding our hand and helping us every moment.

God uses chronic pain and weakness, along with other afflictions, as his chisel for sculpting our lives. Felt weakness deepens dependence on Christ for strength each day. The weaker we feel, the harder we lean. And the harder we lean, the stronger we grow spiritually, even while our bodies waste away.

J. I. Packer

God's strength in your weakness is his presence in your life.

Andy Stanley

God will always be there with us and give us the strength to meet the difficulties of life.

Wendell E. Mettey

For Further Reflection

Jeremiah 17:7-9; Isaiah 26:4; 2 Corinthians 4:16-18

TODAY'S PRAYER

God, I confess, when I am hurting and weak, I look to other things to support me. However, you stand ready to support me in ways that no one and nothing else can. When times are tough, please remind me you are my rock. Amen.

False Guilt

Who will bring any charge against those whom God has chosen? It is God who justifies. Who then is the one who condemns? No one. Christ Jesus who died—more than that, who was raised to life—is at the right hand of God and is also interceding for us.

ROMANS 8:33–34 NIV

Some of us are strongly independent. We can tackle many types of tasks and handle multiple responsibilities successfully. We rarely ask for help. It doesn't matter what the tasks are; we figure out a way to get them done. Other people see us as productive and dependable. They respect and rely on us.

But what happens when we cannot complete our tasks as we used to because we just don't feel like ourselves? What happens when we want help, but something in us prevents us from acknowledging and asking for what we need?

In psychology circles, the inability to ask for help does not mean a person is independent. Instead, it's possible the individual is operating from a place of guilt—false guilt. If we find ourselves resisting the idea of asking for help, perhaps we're feeling a false guilt that we are going to be a burden to the person we are asking. Feelings of false guilt for allowing "this" to happen. Feelings of false guilt that we can't complete the tasks we want to.

To break the pattern of these thoughts, we need to ask ourselves: Is having a need bad? The answer is no. God would not have us hindered by such feelings. He does not want us trying to handle things on our own. It is perfectly okay to ask for help or advice. We were created for community, and the Bible talks about how we are to serve one another. One of the best things we can learn to do for ourselves is to recognize false guilt, reframe those thoughts to more accurate statements, and ask for help.

As you go through life, don't let your feelings—real as they are—invalidate your need to let the truth of God's words guide your thinking. Remember that the path to your heart travels through your mind. Truth matters.

Randy Alcorn

To meditate on Scripture is to allow the truth of God's Word to move from head to heart. It is to so dwell upon a truth that it becomes part of our being.

Greg Oden

For Further Reflection

Galatians 6:2; Philippians 2:4; 1 Thessalonians 5:11

TODAY'S PRAYER

Lord, you are the only one who is self-sufficient. You created me to live in community and rely on the body to be your hands and feet. Please help me to remember to reach out. Amen.

Healing Is a Process

*There is a season (a time appointed) for everything
and a time for every delight and event
or purpose under heaven.*

ECCLESIASTES 3:1 AMP

There is no doubt that healing is a process. If we skin our knees, it takes a few days for the red blood cells to do their things and connect with the right tissue to seal the break. If we break a bone, it takes time for a callus to form around the broken bone and develop new bone growth. Emotional wounds can be a little different.

Healing is a process. Some people take short cuts in an effort to make it happen faster. Others give up altogether. Either way, healing is delayed or never happens. One thing that can help bring peace and encouragement during times of trial is accepting that instant healing might not be what Jesus has for us. The ten lepers were healed as they were going (Luke 17:11-19). The blind man had to wash in the pool of Siloam before his sight was restored (John 9:1-11).

Stories of how some people heal quickly or instantly are exciting, but they are also the exception. For most people, true healing takes time and effort. Often healing is a journey, and one that does not lie in a straight line or across flat terrain. Healing could be days or months of progress and setbacks. The fact that the process is taking longer than we think it should does not mean we are on the wrong path or we should give up. Just the contrary! Healing only comes if we are willing to move forward as best we can toward what we know will be beneficial to us.

Change, like healing, takes time.

Veronica Roth

There are far better things ahead than any we leave behind.

C. S. Lewis

But more often than not, real recovery is slow. It takes time. And the deeper the wound, the more extensive the damage or trauma, the greater amount of time may be required for us to recover.

Chuck Swindoll

For Further Reflection

Philippians 1:6; James 1:4; Hebrews 10:36

TODAY'S PRAYER

Lord, I admit that I grow impatient waiting for healing. I don't understand why some people have been healed, yet you have not healed me. Please help me to focus on the process you are walking me through, for nothing will be wasted. Amen.

God's Good Heart

Taste and see that the LORD is good;
blessed is the one who takes refuge in him.

PSALM 34:8

We all experience times when the difficulties seem to keep piling up. Maybe we had a recent surgery and within a couple of weeks, the doctors tell us the procedure did not work and it needs to be repeated. We just start to recover from the surgery when someone in our family catches the flu and they need us to provide meals. At the same time, we experience a relationship breakup or a job loss. Individual events can start to accumulate and drive us to discouragement.

When physical, financial, emotional, or relational problems keep striking, we can start to question God and his plans. We might start to doubt that God is good and question how goodness could come out of such discomfort or troubles.

Hopefully we can be honest about our thoughts and feelings with people we trust and confide in. We might simply need someone to sit and listen to us and help us focus on God and be reminded of his attributes. When we are in despair, it can be difficult to keep our spiritual focus. Instead we get caught up in the tangible things and focus on our present pain and hardships.

Realizing that God is in control and that his ways are always right (whether we like the circumstances or not) will help us in our faith journey. No matter what we are going through, our faith is strengthened when we choose to see our circumstances through the lens of God's truth and goodness.

The worldling blesses God while he gives him plenty, but the Christian blesses him when he smites him: he believes him to be too wise to err and too good to be unkind; he trusts him where he cannot trace him, looks up to him in the darkest hour, and believes that all is well.

Charles Spurgeon

The goodness of God is infinitely more wonderful than we will ever be able to comprehend.

A. W. Tozer

We should be astonished at the goodness of God, stunned that he should bother to call us by name, our mouths wide open at his love, bewildered that at this very moment we are standing on holy ground.

Brennan Manning

For Further Reflection

1 Chronicles 16:34; Psalm 69:1; James 1:17

TODAY'S PRAYER

Father, day after day you have proven to me that you are good. Even when I don't understand what you are doing, please help me to remember that you are that same good Father. Amen.

DAY 61

Waving the White Flag

*Take your everyday, ordinary life—your sleeping,
eating, going-to-work, and walking-around life—
and place it before God as an offering.*

ROMANS 12:1 MSG

The white flag has long been a symbol of truce. In war, many have used the recognizable technique of waving a white flag to communicate a willingness to start peace talks, offer concessions, begin negotiations, or collect the wounded. The person carrying the white flag is not supposed to attack, and they are not to be attacked, as they are in the position of surrender.

When faced with a difficult situation, we often want to fight our way through it, relying on our own limited knowledge and resources. However, as we prepare to face our battle against depression, we can choose instead to wave the white flag of surrender to God. Surrendering the struggle to God does not mean we give up or give in, but rather we give over to what God has for us during this time. It means we are leaving the future of this particular journey in God's hands. It means we hand over our desire to manage it all on our own.

When we surrender to God, we are putting our faith in him and in his promises. It is a choice. It looks very much like what children do when adults reassure them that we will meet their needs. Children give an "okay" of acknowledgment, smile, and go back to playing. No hint of doubt. No attempt to try to retake control. No second-guessing.

We can have that same faith—the faith of a child. We too can wave the white flag to surrender to God our depression, our treatment, and the outcome. Then we can get back in the game of life.

In our abandonment we give ourselves over to God just as God gave Himself for us, without any calculations. The consequences of abandonment never enter into our outlook because our life is taken up in Him.

Oswald Chambers

God is ready to assume full responsibility for the life wholly yielded to Him.

Andrew Murray

You become stronger only when you become weaker. When you surrender your will to God, you discover the resources to do what God requires.

Erwin Lutzer

For Further Reflection

Luke 9:23-24; Luke 14:23; Philippians 3:8

TODAY'S PRAYER

Lord, please help me to surrender all of my life to you. And when I start to feel like you need my help, please remind me to surrender again. Amen.

Peace in Unsettled Times

Peace I leave with you, my peace I give you. I do not give to you as the world gives. Do not let your hearts be troubled and do not be afraid.

JOHN 14:27

Picture walking through the tunnel to board a plane. You're excited. The roar of engines grows louder. You're greeted by a flight attendant who welcomes you aboard. You find your seat, stow your carry-on, put on our seat belt and wait for takeoff. During the flight, the plane cuts through the clouds and turns toward the sun. Sometimes you can see the snowcapped mountains or rivers below. *Peace.*

Twenty minutes into the flight, you feel a sudden jostle. The mood of the passengers changes at the cabin's uneven movements. The fasten seatbelt sign flashes and ... *ding.* The pilot comes on the intercom explaining that the plane has encountered turbulence, and the pilot advises the flight attendants to take their seats. What started as a calm beautiful flight became a very unsettling journey.

When we receive a new mental health diagnosis, the news can throw life into turbulent cycle. Our behaviors might become impulsive as we attempt to find relief or a different diagnosis. Our minds spin with many questions needing answers. But no matter what the circumstances are, Jesus wants us to have peace in him (John 16:33). Just as the seatbelt on the plane can give us a sense of peace, remembering that Jesus is aware of our circumstances and that he is with us can be our seatbelt of peace.

Rather than shrinking in fear and despondency, we can lean in to God's presence while taking steps to adjust to our new reality. Remembering God is in control can help calm our hearts and bring peace. Regardless of how bumpy the journey may be, God will deliver us to our final destination. Therefore, we have nothing to fear.

When trouble comes, focus on God's ability to care for you.

Charles Stanley

Sometimes the Lord rides out the storm with us and other times he calms the restless sea around us. Most of all, he calms the storm inside us in our deepest inner soul.

Lloyd John Ogilvie

A great many people are trying to make peace, but that has already been done. God has not left it for us to do; all we have to do—is to enter into it.

Dwight L. Moody

For Further Reflection

Psalm 62:2; Acts 2:25; Psalm 91:14-15

TODAY'S PRAYER

Heavenly Father, as I face today and the challenges that may come, please help me face them boldly. Teach me how to see these challenges as an opportunity to grow in you for your name's sake. Amen.

Hope 'til the End

And we desire for each one of you to show the same diligence [all the way through] so as to realize and enjoy the full assurance of hope until the end.

HEBREWS 6:11 AMP

So many times in life we experience things that bring us to a point of hopelessness. In that state, our perception can be skewed and our mood deflated. If we add the complications of depression, we want to quit. We see no way out or no positive change. We resign to our circumstances, believing this is all there is. We enter the dark tunnel with no light at the end.

To have hope is to want something better for our life, even if it is in the smallest measure. Having hope can help us in the moment, but it also motivates us to keep going. Hope can open our eyes to new possibilities and propel us forward even though we may feel like nothing is changing. Hope is expectation of a positive outcome. And for the Christian believer, we have an expectation greater than ourselves or any circumstance—the Lord Jesus Christ.

Hebrews 6:11 communicates that we should never give up! The verse states emphatically that we can always expect a positive outcome, no matter how much difficulty we face, and no matter how long it takes. We can see our desired outcome come into fruition. See healing? Yes. See wholeness restored? Yes. How can we be so sure? Because our expectations are based on our faith in God's promises.

Many of us can be tempted to give up. But with faith in Christ, we can actively carry on. If we know we are headed in the right direction, we are taking care of the parts of our health we can influence and leaving the rest to God. By following the guidance of God's Word, being led by the Holy Spirit and following the recommendations of professionals, we have hope—enough hope—until the end.

Hope is the thing with feathers that perches in the soul and sings the tune without the words and never stops at all.

Emily Dickinson

Hope is being able to see that there is light despite all of the darkness.

Desmond Tutu

The very least you can do in your life is figure out what you hope for. And the most you can do is live inside that hope. Not admire it from a distance but live right in it, under its roof.

Barbara Kingsolver

For Further Reflection

Psalm 42:11; 1 Thessalonians 3:2-4;Hebrews 11:1

TODAY'S PRAYER

Father, you are my only hope. Please help me to do my part, day by day, until I am healed. I thank you that because of you I will always have hope. Amen.

Faith in Action

Don't fool yourself into thinking that you are a listener
when you are anything but, letting the Word go in one
ear and out the other. Act on what you hear! Those
who hear and don't act are like those who glance
in the mirror, walk away, and two minutes later
have no idea who they are, what they look like.

JAMES 1:22 MSG

O ur faith is tested every day, whether in small ways or more impactful ways such as ongoing depression. When we are tested, we demonstrate by our actions if we truly believe what we say about God. We prove whether we can walk the talk.

James 2:17 states, "Faith by itself, if it is not accompanied by action, is dead." Another way of expressing this is that faith all by itself is dormant or inactive, like a seed. We might *believe* that with proper planting and nutrition, the seed will sprout and grow, but actually planting and watering the seed are the *actions* that back up our belief.

For those of us who struggle with depression, we might be in the phase between the belief and the action. Or we may have watered our healing seed and are just waiting for it to bud and leaf. Either way, to see what God has planned for us on this journey, we must put our faith into action. Not only must we continue to believe that God is good and still in control, we must also act on our faith. We must do our part and water our seeds.

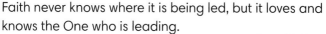

Faith never knows where it is being led, but it loves and knows the One who is leading.

Oswald Chambers

True faith manifests itself through our actions.

Francis Chan

A faith that hasn't been tested can't be trusted.

Adrian Rogers

For Further Reflection

Hebrews 11:1-40; James 2:14-17; 2 Corinthians 5:7

TODAY'S PRAYER

Lord, I know that I can trust you and believe in you. When I feel like you are prompting me in a certain direction, please help me to act on that prompting, knowing that you will lead me. Amen.

The Morning Watch

Now if the firstfruits offered up are holy, so is the whole batch. And if the root is holy, so are the branches.

ROMANS 11:16 HCSB

The morning hours can feel almost sacred. It is the beginning of the day, before family members wake up, before schools and stores are open, and before the cars and trucks get on the roads and highways. For the person who struggles with feelings of sadness or depression, the morning hours can be a struggle. Before we've even opened our eyes, we might have already begun to think and worry, thereby setting the tone for the day. But spending even a few moments with God during those early morning hours can bring us tremendous blessings and provide new strength to face the day ahead.

Time with God might be the last thing some of us want to hear about when we're struggling with depression. We don't feel like spending time in our Bibles or in prayer. But by starting the day with him, we align ourselves with God and his plans for us. We might not agree with the circumstances we find ourselves in, but we can agree with the One who allowed those circumstances and will bring about a healing for his glory and in his timing.

Why is morning a good time to spend moments with God? Because it is a time before anything else gets in the way. When we awake, we should take a minute—pause before we face the symptoms that slow us down—to acknowledge that God has given us another day. The time with him is just a moment to look at ourselves in God's mirror (symptoms and all!), and see ourselves as God sees us. Doing this can set the right tone for the day, regardless of our initial mood.

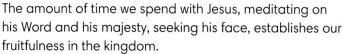

The amount of time we spend with Jesus, meditating on his Word and his majesty, seeking his face, establishes our fruitfulness in the kingdom.

Charles Stanley

Ten minutes spent in the presence of Christ every day, aye, two minutes, will make the whole day different.

William Henry Drummond

I ought to pray before seeing any one. …Christ arose before day and went into a solitary place. David says: "Early will I seek thee."… I feel it is far better to begin with God—to see his face first, to get my soul near him before it is near another.

Robert Murray M'Cheyne

For Further Reflection

Psalm 5:3; Psalm 88:13; Psalm 143:8

TODAY'S PRAYER

Lord, getting out of bed is challenging enough. Each day as you wake me, please help me to remember to acknowledge you, even if it's simply with a "good morning." Amen.

Look Up!

I lift my eyes up to the mountains—
where does my help come from?

Psalm 121:1

In the movie *The Lord of the Rings: The Two Towers*, the final battle takes place in a valley called Helm's Deep. The army of Rohan and the Rohirrim (the good guys) retreat into the fortress for protection against an attack of the Orcs and Dunlendings (the bad guys). The good guys hold off the bad guys all night by launching their defenses from the rooftops of the fortress. In the morning as the bad guys breech the fortress gates, the battle horn sounds. The king and the heir to the throne decide to lead what they believe will be their final ride, thinking they will at least go down fighting. As they charge out of the fortress to face the Orcs and the Dunlendings, they look up. Atop the adjoining hill appears a lone white horse ridden by Gandalf the Grey (good guy). He is accompanied by enough reinforcements to scare away the bad guys.

What a story! Just when things seem at their worst, they look up and see their help. The book of Psalms gives us parallel imagery. Psalm 121:1 begins, "I lift my eyes to the mountains—where does my help come from?" The answer is in the next verse: "My help comes from the Lord, the Maker of heaven and earth."

We might be facing insurmountable odds. We might be surrounded on all sides by injury, loss, sadness, or depression. Despite these trials, we have to remember that

God is always ready and available to help us. Our focus needs to be on God who is our only source of help. When we're feeling overwhelmed and discouraged, it's all right to stop and say aloud, "Look up!"

God's work done in God's way will never lack God's supplies.

Hudson Taylor

God will meet you where you are in order to take you where he wants you to go.

Tony Evans

Safety comes in our nearness to God, not in our distance from our enemies.

Dillon Burroughs

For Further Reflection

Luke 21:28; Titus 2:13; Jude 14

TODAY'S PRAYER

When I feel like I am surrounded on all sides with no help in sight, help me to look up. Amen.

Waiting

Then King David went in and sat before the Lord.

2 SAMUEL 7:18 ESV

Why would God do this to me? When will I feel better?

These questions often pop up when we're faced with chronic mental distress. Some people, in their effort to explain the unexplainable, say we just need more faith. This incorrect response puts the blame on us, implying that if we had more faith, we would have the healing we hope for. Just as confusing is when we hear about someone else's healing or recovery. Why didn't God choose me? Did I do something wrong?

All great questions without simple answers. The reasons for God's actions or inactions often remain a mystery. In this life, we may never fully know why God allows certain things to happen. We will never know all the reasons why some suffer from depression and others do not. But we do know his ultimate purpose is to bring glory to himself. And we know that the road to healing is a road we take in faith. One of our stops along the road is to find the right care or support group. Another stop is waiting on God.

But let's admit it: we don't like waiting. Waiting doesn't feel natural. We are ready for our healing now. We want to move forward. The busyness that calls to us is the opposite of the quiet waiting that God often asks of us. But in the waiting we receive what we truly want and need—more of God. We learn more about his nature, power, and sovereignty. Waiting provides the opportunity for our hearts to be refreshed by the Holy Spirit, to spend more time in his presence.

So, while we wait for God to answer our prayers for healing or restoration, we can be patient and expectant. God is faithful and he will answer.

All things come to him who waits—provided he knows what he is waiting for.

Woodrow T. Wilson

Biblically, waiting is not just something we have to do until we get what we want. Waiting is part of the process of becoming what God wants us to be.

John Ortberg

If any are inclined to despond, because they do not have such patience, let them be of good courage. It is in the course of our feeble and very imperfect waiting that God Himself, by his hidden power, strengthens us and works out in us the patience of the great saints, the patience of Christ Himself.

Andrew Murray

For Further Reflection

Psalm 27:13–14; Psalm 62:1; Psalm 130:5

TODAY'S PRAYER

Along my journey, please help me to wait well. Please remind me that waiting is a part of the road I travel.

Amen.

I Am Not Forgotten

But even the hairs of your head are all numbered.

MATTHEW 10:30 ESV

We are on the mind of the one who created the heavens and the earth, the God who told the mountains to come this high and the waters to stop there. Those words and images can bring such comfort and help us to rest in peace as we live our lives.

Facing the storms of life can be difficult from any perspective. We can be thinking that we have no idea how we are going to make it through. But as challenging as life may be, we need to remember that we are not alone. God is with us always and sees our pain. Hebrews 2:17–18 says that Jesus was "fully human in every way" and understands the experiences we go through. Nothing happens without him knowing all the details.

For those who struggle with ailments, it sure can feel like God has forgotten us. The truth is that he is right beside us. He is sitting with us in our therapy sessions. He is in line with us at the pharmacy. He is in the room when our depression is so bad we can't get out of bed. He is even there when we feel nothing.

When we start feeling as though we've been forgotten by God, we have some choices. We can become angry and bitter and turn inward, away from God, relying on our own power to resolve our challenges. Or we can go back to Scripture that reminds us of who we are in Christ. We are written on the palm of his hand. We are his children.

God knows both your name and address.

Michelle McKinney Hammond

The devil knows your name but calls you by your sin. God knows your sin but calls you by your name.

Ricardo Sanchez

God's heart is especially tender toward the downtrodden and the defeated. He knows your name and he has seen every tear you have shed.

James Dobson

For Further Reflection

1 Corinthians 8:3; Hebrews 4:13; Exodus 33:17

TODAY'S PRAYER

Heavenly Father, please help me to remember you know my name. Your Word says you call me by name and you sing and dance over me. Amen.

Finding and Taking Advice

The way of a fool is right in his own eyes,
but a wise man listens to advice.

PROVERBS 12:15 ESV

When we're struggling with depression, we might find it difficult to reach out for guidance. But the Bible has many verses regarding the benefits of seeking counsel and accepting advice. Without wisdom, we can suffer setbacks and delay our healing journey.

When we seek guidance, we should look to someone who can speak biblical truth. When we seek medical advice, we want to hear from someone who has trained and practiced in the area in which we are struggling. When we look for community support, we should seek people who are further along their journey than we are. Someone who has not walked in our shoes might be able to offer a different perspective that we might not have considered.

Although we might seek and receive biblical guidance, we can still refuse to apply it. We might choose not to follow the advice because of pride, or simply believing we can trust ourselves to know what is best. The Bible speaks of the danger of going down this path. Proverbs 28:26 says, "Whoever trusts in his own mind is a fool, but he who walks in wisdom will be delivered."

The most important test of counsel is to compare it against Scripture. Any advice contrary to the Bible is troublesome.

We can also compare new advice to the body of knowledge we already know to be solid.

Philippians 1:9-10 states, "And this is my prayer: that your love may abound more and more in knowledge and depth of insight, so that you may be able to discern what is best and may be pure and blameless for the day of Christ." One of God's desires for us is that we grow in wisdom and discernment.

He that won't be counseled can't be helped.

Benjamin Franklin

A wise man seeks much counsel ... a fool listens to all of it.

Larry Burkett

One of the primary reasons we don't seek counsel from the wise people around us is that we already know what we are going to hear and we just don't want to hear it.

Andy Stanley

For Further Reflection

James 1:5; Proverbs 3:13-18; Proverbs 1:5;
Proverbs 19:20

TODAY'S PRAYER

Father, please help me to seek, listen to, and apply godly wisdom, even if it isn't easy. Give me the wisdom to discern my next steps. Amen.

The Power of Thought

Finally, brothers, whatever is true, whatever is honorable,
whatever is just, whatever is pure, whatever is lovely,
whatever is commendable, if there is any excellence, if
there is anything worthy of praise, think about these things.

PHILIPPIANS 4:8 ESV

Our brains are more powerful than the top scientists can understand. Despite years of developmental science, we have not unraveled the mystery of the brain. The brain, with each segment playing its own role, coordinates our behaviors, responses, and feelings. In a perfect brain, all systems function as intended, with all chemicals at the appropriate levels. We know that sometimes circumstances outside our control affect the functioning of our brain. However, even in those situations, we can work to bring our thought life under Christ's control.

English philosopher James Allen said, "As a man thinks, so he is; as he continues to think, so he remains." What we think about and focus on can affect our perception of who we are and ultimately our behaviors. Our thought life is interconnected with other areas of our life. Consider this example: If we believe our depression is a hopeless situation and no one understands, we can become discouraged, feel useless, and grow more depressed. If we keep focusing on those negative thoughts, those feelings increase. We might withdraw further. We might not share when we have a need. We might not seek professional help. Our thoughts have created a downward spiral.

But if we encourage thoughts that are more realistic, our outcome will be better. We can acknowledge that living with depression is difficult, but we can also recognize that many others have experienced a similar diagnosis, and many have recovered. We don't have to feel isolated or without hope. By directing our thoughts differently, we will be more likely to share our experience and get the assistance we need.

God's Word tells us to "take every thought captive to obey Christ" (2 Corinthians 10:5 ESV) To break the cycle of negative thoughts, we have to recognize them, challenge them, and reframe as appropriate. Our mental health depends on it.

Life consists mainly of the storm of thoughts that is forever flowing through one's head.

Mark Twain

A man's life is what his thoughts make of it.

Marcus Aurelius

When a negative thought goes unchallenged, your mind believes it and your body reacts to it.

Dr. Daniel Amen

For Further Reflection

Romans 12:2; Proverbs 4:23; Colossians 3:2-5

TODAY'S PRAYER

Father, thank you for how the mind works. Please help me to recognize thoughts that do not honor you and to replace them with your words. Amen.

The Rearview Mirror

Jesus replied, "No one who puts a hand to the plow and looks back is fit for service in the kingdom of God."

LUKE 9:62

Reflecting on the past can help us make wiser choices in the future; however, living in the past is one way to increase depression, because we are focusing on something we cannot change. We know the past can't be changed. Yet how many of us meditate on decisions we've made, things we've said, places we've gone? Sometimes when we ruminate, we can feel as though the memory is squeezing the life out of us. In a sense, it is. Instead of paying attention to where we're going, we're looking in the rearview mirror at things gone by.

Making peace with the past isn't easy. We have to express our pain and face the truth as best we can. We might need help to deal with the pain. As we process our memories, our support team can help us stay focused on the present while identifying what is preventing us from moving forward. While we process, we also learn new skills and different ways of silencing the thoughts that condemn us. We can then embrace the present and future with a solid foundation of forgiveness and peace.

The process of working through the past might not be in a straight line. We might think a hurt is resolved, but then something brings up old thoughts and emotions. That's okay. Acknowledge them, and move on. The goal is to keep moving forward. As we do so, that painful past will grow smaller in comparison to the present and future. God wants us to focus on him and his plans for us. Someone once said there is a reason why the rearview mirror is small and the windshield is so much bigger.

Getting over a painful experience is much like crossing monkey bars. You have to let go at some point in order to move forward.

C. S. Lewis

The beautiful journey of today can only begin when you learn to let go of yesterday.

Steve Maraboli

When one door closes, another opens; but we often look so long and so regretfully upon the closed door that we do not see the one which has opened for us.

Alexander Graham Bell

For Further Reflection

Matthew 6:14; Romans 12:19; Ephesians 4:26–27

TODAY'S PRAYER

Lord, help me to reflect on the past as a reference point to remind where I've come from. Please help me to forgive myself and others so I am free to move forward. Amen.

Trusting He's Got You

But you will not leave in haste or go in flight;
for the LORD will go before you, the God
of Israel will be your rear guard.

ISAIAH 52:12

I magine skydiving. Picture yourself standing at an open doorway of an aircraft. The adrenaline is pumping. You're surrounded by professionals who have done this hundreds of times. They're all smiles. At the right time, you drop out of the plane into the sky with the instructor attached, descending at a rate of 100 miles per hour, if not more. As the earth rushes up, the instructor looks at his wrist altimeter and at a specific moment pulls a cord. You drift side to side and aim for a designated spot to end the journey. As your air speed slows, you catch your breath and start to enjoy the scenic views. Clouds. Mountains. The different shades of the terrain. Without someone pulling the cord, you would be accelerating too quickly and miss the view of the earth and sky from this height. But when the cord was pulled, the parachute caught you, allowing a more controlled decent to your destination.

After we initially receive a diagnosis, we might feel as if we're free-falling. We struggle to understand what the doctor is saying. We try to come up with sensible questions. We nod as if we comprehend the doctor's statements, but as soon as we step out the office door, life rushes at us as we try to digest what this information means for our future.

If we're followers of Christ, God stands ready to catch us. As we free-fall in a haze of confusion, God catches us and guides us to a safe landing. Some days it might feel as though our symptoms are battering us, blowing us randomly across the landscape of life. But our instructor and guide has us in the grip of his hand.

The strong hands of God twisted the crown of thorns into a crown of glory; and in such hands we are safe.

Charles Williams

Adversity is always unexpected and unwelcomed. It is an intruder and a thief. But in the hands of God, adversity becomes the means through which his supernatural power is demonstrated.

Charles Stanley

Destiny waits in the hand of God, not in the hands of statesmen.

T. S. Eliot

For Further Reflection

John 14:16–18; Deuteronomy 31:8; Isaiah 41:10

TODAY'S PRAYER

Lord, thank you for always having my back,
for always catching me when I jump. As I face
this new trail, please help me remember you still
have my back. Amen.

Do Not Forget

*Remember [carefully] the former things [which I did]
from ages past; For I am God, and there is no one else;
I am God, and there is no one like Me.*

Isaiah 46:9 AMP

Have you ever noticed repeated words or phrases in the Bible? Over the years, we may have heard about how many times the word fear or love appears in the Bible. Repetition helps emphasize a point and helps the listener recall something important. Sometimes certain phrases are repeated in the same chapter or verse. One key command word that is repeated throughout scripture is remember.

In the Old Testament, the word remember appears between 121–137 times (depending on the Bible translation). To remember means "to recall to the mind by an act or effort; to have something come into the mind again."[8] And "to have something come to mind again" requires that we recognize something in the first place. In Deuteronomy 4:9, God used Moses to command the Israelites to bring to mind again all the ways they had seen God work on their behalf. The act of remembering provided a time for thanksgiving but it was also important during times of suffering, when life was not going as smoothly as anticipated.

The same command applies to us. When we take time to bring to mind again all the things the Lord has done for us, brought us through, healed us from, we will be strengthened in the current circumstance, knowing that God is still our provider. In biblical times, God's people built standing stones or pillars so the current generation could mark a time and place where

God watched over them. The standing stones also served as a marker for foreigners who traveled through the land, so they might come to know the significance of the stones.

Throughout our lives, during times of blessing as well as trial, what standing stones have we erected as markers of how God has taken care of us?

Sometimes, to overcome a hurdle before us, we don't need to search for new truth or understanding of God so much as we need to live out what we already know.

Amy Layne Litzelman

Remembering God's work in the past has a sustaining and renewing effect during times of spiritual drought. Memory and worship are thus keys to a long life of spiritual formation.

Richard J. Foster

We survive the packages for pain God allows in our lives by remembering who God is and what he has done in the past.

Linda Dillow

For Further Reflection

Exodus 13:3; Psalm 77:11; Psalm 143:5

TODAY'S PRAYER

Lord, your track record in my life has been perfect. As I face this new challenge, please help me to remember your reputation. Amen.

Access to God

*This is the confidence we have in approaching God: that
if we ask anything according to his will, he hears us.*

1 JOHN 5:14

Technology is a blessing in so many ways. The ease at which we have access to friends and family has increased over the years. With the click of a button, we have access to what is happening in people's lives. Certain platforms might make us feel popular because we have "followers." We can interact in chat rooms, share photos, and instantly connect with people all over the globe. Technological advancements have made us easily accessible any time, day or night.

Such easy accessibility has some downsides. Sometimes we forget the passwords to get into the accounts and we must jump through security hoops to get reconnected. If we forget to renew a subscription to certain services, we might lose the ability to contact others. Differing time zones can create communication challenges. We can also experience fatigue from excessive social media in our lives.

It is not so with God. He does not set his availability by day or time. There is no designated place with a good signal. There are no dues or fees required to receive a connection. The voicemail box is never full. And God most certainly never grows weary of us. If we proclaim Jesus as our Lord and Savior, we have immediate access to him. We can pray. Sing praises. Meditate on his Word to learn more of him.

Sometimes when we are feeling our worst, reaching out to people is difficult. Or sometimes people might not be available. But God is always accessible and ready to hear us.

God does nothing except in response to believing prayer.

John Wesley

Prayer is the means of sustaining a faith that at times can grow weak. The power of prayer is enriching, uplifting to hear our God speak.

Greta Zwaan

For Further Reflection

Psalm 121:4; Ephesians 3:12; Psalm 91:15

TODAY'S PRAYER

God, thank you that you know and hear my voice. Thank you that you stand ready to respond in grace and mercy. Help me to never forget you are there. Amen.

Never Alone

*For I am convinced that neither death nor life, neither
angels nor demons, neither the present nor the future,
nor any powers, neither height nor depth, nor anything
else in all creation, will be able to separate us from the
love of God that is in Christ Jesus our Lord.*

ROMANS 8:38–39

It is easy to shift from our secure foundation in Christ when life is not going as planned and we face difficult decisions. We do all the right things—pray, worship, seek wise counsel—but God doesn't seem to respond. The silence seems more acute when we are expecting to hear something so that we can move forward, and we don't. Often, we move confidently through life, making decisions because we feel sure-footed. We might not be even trying to hear God's voice or see God's hand. But when we are looking for direction from him and don't see it, we recognize the silence and believe we are alone.

But we are never alone. How do we know? God promised several times in the Bible that he will never leave us or forsake us. God has assured us of his faithful presence. We might go through situations that make us feel like we are alone, but we must remember what Scripture says and choose to believe what God has already told us. This is part of the faith journey. Despite what we see, feel, or hear, we rely on what Scripture tells us, trusting that God knows where we are and what we are experiencing.

We are never alone, because nothing can separate us from the love of God: not depression, not sadness, not loneliness, not days in isolation, not over-sleeping, not anxiety, and not any diagnosis. We always have God's presence. We never walk alone.

God, who is everywhere, never leaves us. Yet he seems sometimes to be present, sometimes to be absent. If we do not know him well, we do not realize that he may be more present to us when he is absent than when he is present.

Thomas Merton

Your presence fills every space of a heart that seeks to find; your love is here to save us and your name is love defined.

Lisa Mischelle Wood

Having the reality of God's presence is not dependent on our being in a particular circumstance or place, but is only dependent on our determination to keep the Lord before us continually.

Oswald Chambers

For Further Reflection

Psalm 139:7; Matthew 1:23; Joshua 1:9; Isaiah 43:2

TODAY'S PRAYER

God, I thank you that you are always by my side. Please forgive me for the times that I assumed you left me and took matters into my own hands. Amen.

In for the Long Haul

For we are his workmanship [his own master work,
a work of art], created in Christ Jesus [reborn from
above—spiritually transformed, renewed, ready to be
used] for good works, which God prepared [for us]
beforehand [taking paths which he set], so that we
would walk in them [living the good life which
he prearranged and made ready for us].

EPHESIANS 2:10 AMP

We all have moments of being up and down, sad or happy, or not feeling like ourselves. Sometimes it is the result of the circumstances we find ourselves in. Other times we cannot explain it. Unfortunately, there is no way to predict how long we will struggle with our symptoms. However, our lives do not have to be controlled by the ever-changing whim of symptoms. No matter how long we find ourselves sitting in depressive feelings, God wants us to care for ourselves. By doing so, we can have full, meaningful lives, good relationships, and clear thinking.

In Exodus 18, Moses finds himself trying to manage the newly freed Israelites. His roles are many, including governor, judge, jury, and mediator. His days are long and full of conversations regarding matters great and small. Jethro, Moses's father-in-law, comes for a visit and witnesses Moses's duties. He tells Moses, "What you are doing is not good. You and these people who come to you will only wear yourselves out" (verses 17–18). In other words, you can't keep this up. Jethro then educates Moses regarding how to take care of himself and the people of Israel.

We too need to be educated on how to care for ourselves so that we can live productive lives while we are feeling depressed. This may mean learning about depression. It may mean we investigate possible remedies, including long or short term prescriptions. It may mean we need to process negative emotions by crying or beginning a grief process. With God's leading, we can become the best advocates for our self-care, enabling us to be available and prepared for the work God has called us to do.

Talk to yourself like you would to someone you love.

Brené Brown

Rest and self-care are so important. When you take time to replenish your spirit, it allows you to serve others from the overflow. You cannot serve from an empty vessel.

Eleanor Brownn

Self-care has become a new priority—the revelation that it's perfectly permissible to listen to your body and do what it needs.

Frances Ryan

For Further Reflection
Ephesians 5:29; 1 Corinthians 6:19–20; 3 John 1:2

TODAY'S PRAYER

Father, thank you for being with me on this journey.
I admit that I am not at my best to serve you or
anyone else. Please help me to find the right
balance along my healing journey. Amen.

The Low Point

He lifted me out of the slimy pit, out of the
mud and mire; he set my feet on a rock
and gave me a firm place to stand.

PSALM 40:2

Sometimes the low point can come out of nowhere. It might be a sudden, radical change in what we thought life was going to be like. We are so surprised that we do not know where to turn. Other times, the change is a gradual decent into paralysis. We knew we weren't doing well, but we thought we had a handle on things. Then before we realize it, we hit such a dark and difficult time, we truly believe it can't get any worse.

Then God shows up and rescues us.

Psalm 40:1–5 records a low point of David's life when he cried out to the Lord who rescued him. It is not clear exactly when David wrote this psalm because his life was full of dark moments. Regardless, David remembers that God brought him up from "the slimy pit" and "the mud and mire." The imagery of God reaching down and lifting David out of the pit and setting him on the rocks above is riveting. David then says that because of his rescue, he is able to sing again.

If we struggle with depression or despondency, we know that our pits may not be a one-time thing. Psalm 40 starting at verse 11 records David's request for continued help because he knows there will be other times when he is in the pit. Just like David, we can remember what God has done for us in the past and at our next low point remind ourselves that God is the one who rescues us from the pits.

God takes care of his own. He knows our needs. He anticipates our crises. He is moved by our weaknesses. He stands ready to come to our rescue. And at just the right moment, he steps in and proves Himself as our faithful heavenly Father.

Chuck Swindoll

God is on the move to rescue people from misery to everlasting happiness, which can only be found in him.

John Piper

God does not stop at rescuing us; the purpose of that rescue is to enjoy fellowship with us.

A. W. Tozer

For Further Reflection

Psalm 82:3-4; Psalm 17:6; Psalm 18:2

TODAY'S PRAYER

Lord, thank you for meeting me where I am. Thank you that I am never out of your reach. Please help me to remember that you always hear my cry. Amen.

Our Focus

Let your eyes look straight ahead;
fix your gaze directly before you.

PROVERBS 4:25

Have you ever tried to teach someone how to ride a bike? It can be terrifying to watch as they learn how to steer and keep their balance. There might be more instances of veering off the path than there are of staying on the path. But the one thing they may not realize immediately is this: Where they focus their eyes or head is where they will go.

Consider learning how to drive a car. You'll hear, "Eyes on the road!" Why? Because the car starts to drift in the direction we look. It's amazing how such a small shift in our focus can deter us from the path that is better for us.

The same holds true when we are not feeling like ourselves. Our symptoms can derail us from the healthier things we need to do (or used to do), and ultimately prevent us from focusing on God. It's not intentional, but it can sneak up on us as we struggle in our own strength to manage our symptoms. We have somehow gotten so off track that we forget to seek God and we have run off the road.

The good news is that even in the middle of our most difficult times, we can refocus our attention and our minds on God and he will bring us back to the right path. Because he is always with us, he is there to answer when we ask for help, and gently helps us refocus. It may not mean our symptoms go away, but it does mean we never have to walk alone when our eyes are fixed on him.

Even when it feels as if we are being crushed by earthly troubles, we can remain joyful. If we keep our focus on God, our spirit cannot be trampled.

Mary C. Neal

Instead of concentrating on your problems and getting discouraged, focus on God and meditate on His promises for you. You may have fallen down, but you don't have to stay down. God is ready, willing and able to pick you up.

Joyce Meyer

Vision is the ability to see God's presence, to perceive God's power, to focus on God's plan in spite of the obstacles.

Chuck Swindoll

For Further Reflection

Colossians 3:2; 1 Corinthians 10:31; Proverbs 3:6

TODAY'S PRAYER

Lord, I can't figure out why or how I have these depressive feelings. But I know that I can call on your name and you will meet me wherever I am. And when you meet me where I am, you will lift my head and help me refocus. Please help me to remember that. Amen.

The Voice from on High

*When the righteous cry for help, the LORD hears and
delivers them out of all their troubles. The LORD is near
to the brokenhearted and saves the crushed in spirit.*

PSALM 34:17–18 ESV

Sometimes we don't realize we are on the road to
depression until we arrive. Suddenly we look around
but see no familiar street signs or traffic lights. The
scenery looks familiar, yet feels very different. Even the air
is different—heavy and thick. It feels like someone is sitting
on our chest. Or maybe depression feels like we're suddenly
trapped, as if we are at the bottom of a well, enclosed on all
sides. It's dark and tight, and as we reach for the walls to get
some kind of bearing, we can't find our way. We are broken.

Then we look up and see the opening at the top of that well.
We see brightness, maybe the sun, maybe just the blueness
of sky. We catch a whiff of clean air, some relief to our
heaviness. Is it possible there is a way out? We whimper,
"Help?" and wonder if anyone can hear. The answer is yes!

The Lord God who made the heavens and the earth—that
bright expanse that caught our attention at the top of the
well—heard our cry for help. His voice is that small, quiet
whispering that says, "I'm here." The sound captures our
breath. We tear up, not out of sadness but out of relief. He
heard us. He answered us. Our help is on the way.

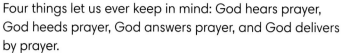

Four things let us ever keep in mind: God hears prayer, God heeds prayer, God answers prayer, and God delivers by prayer.

Edward McKendree Bounds

Our prayers may be awkward. Our attempts may be feeble. But since the power of prayer is in the one who hears it and not in the one who says it, our prayers do make a difference.

Max Lucado

If you believe in prayer at all, expect God to hear you. If you do not expect, you will not have. God will not hear you unless you believe he will hear you; but if you believe he will, he will be as good as your faith.

Charles Spurgeon

For Further Reflection

Hebrews 11:6; 1 John 5:14; Psalm 145:18-19

TODAY'S PRAYER

Lord, I have nothing. I am empty. Will you help me? Your Word says yes. Give me the faith to cry out to you, knowing that you hear me and will answer.

Amen

Get Moving

For while bodily training is of some value, godliness is of value in every way, as it holds promise for the present life and also for the life to come.

1 Timothy 4:8 esv

Millions of us suffer from depression. Primary care physicians can offer guidance, and one piece of advice at the top of their list is exercise. We might not think it makes sense—we don't feel well, but we are supposed to exercise? And if we exercise, we will feel better? Which comes first?

The answer is, it doesn't really matter. What does matter is that clinical evidence suggests that getting regular exercise—moving regularly with intent—can be beneficial to improving our mood. We already know that regular exercise is good for the body. It's not just about anaerobic activity and muscle building; exercise also produces changes in the brain. Exercising releases chemicals that aid in our overall well-being. When we exercise, our heart gets stronger and our brain function improves. We notice that the heaviness starts to lift and we may even feel happy. Our struggles have not disappeared, but exercising and the physical benefits can be a distraction (a good distraction) in the battle with depression.

Exercising does not have to be a major change in the daily schedule. It can be simply making the decision to move a little. Start small, even with just getting out of bed and stepping outside. Take a deep breath—refresh the air in the lungs. Even just that small action can have a surprising positive effect. The next action could be a walk around the yard or neighborhood (if you have a pet that requires walking, they will help you!). Maybe the movement is dancing to music while vacuuming. The idea is to get the muscles working, increase that heart rate and take deep breaths.

On our darkest days, exercise might be the last thing on our mind. But even a small amount of movement can have a great impact on mental health.

Walking is the best possible exercise. Habituate yourself to walk very far.

Thomas Jefferson

The doctor of the future will give no medicine, but will involve the patient in the proper use of food, fresh air, and exercise.

Thomas Edison

Take care of your body. It's the only place you have to live in.

Jim Rohn

For Further Reflection

1 Corinthians 6:19–20; Ezekiel 47:12; 1 Corinthians 9:27

TODAY'S PRAYER

Dear God, exercising is the last thing I feel like doing. But taking care of your temple (my body) is my responsibility. Thank you for the assurance that you're walking with me each day. Amen.

Good Food for a Good Mood

So whether you eat or drink or whatever you do,
do it all for the glory of God.

1 Corinthians 10:31

The phrase "garbage in, garbage out" expresses the concept that poor data input leads to faulty data output. The same concept applies to food. Studies cited by the Mayo Clinic state that food and the severity of our depression could be related. Food can play a role in our moods. They found that research subjects with diets high in processed foods, sugar, and fat reported higher levels of depressive symptoms.[9]

Conversely, according to the study, subjects with diets high in fiber, fruits, and vegetables were likely to experience lower levels of depressive symptoms. Organizations such as the American Heart Association and Johns Hopkins Medicine recommend certain eating plans such as the Mediterranean diet, which emphasizes fruits and vegetables and limits processed meats and dairy products.[10]

Whatever our dietary preference, we have options that can either harm or help our mood. We can choose foods that make a positive difference in our emotional health and optimize our brain functioning. God made our bodies to interact with the foods we eat. Just as we want to enter good data to provide accurate results, we want to give our bodies good nutrients to enable brain health.

Moderation. Small helpings. Sample a little bit of
everything. These are the secrets of happiness and
good health.

Julia Child

Real food has the power to give you your life back and
more fully engage in the purpose for your life.

Rick Warren

Everything in food works together to create health
or disease. The more we think that a single chemical
characterizes a whole food, the more we stray into idiocy.

Dr. T. Colin Campbell

For Further Reflection

Proverbs 25:27; 1 Corinthians 6:12; Ecclesiastes 3:13

TODAY'S PRAYER

Lord, please help me to wisely examine my diet.
Give me the power to make changes that work
best for your temple. Amen

Sacrificial Thanksgiving

Offer to God a sacrifice of thanksgiving,
and perform your vows to the Most High.

PSALM 50:14 ESV

A road trip is an incredible opportunity to see what is outside our small worlds. A road trip can be a journey with hills and valleys, storms and sunny days, discoveries and special moments. If we are not careful, we can fail to recognize that both parts—the good and the bad—work together to create the adventure and memorable experience. Similar to life.

Life has so much to offer and holds so much promise—moments of joy and happiness that we can celebrate with the people around us. We talk openly about the positive parts, not leaving out any details. In those moments, it's easy to slow down and be grateful for all we have and the people we can share it with.

But life can also be like the rocky stretch up a dark mountain pass. Our path is a slow, constant upward toil that strains the engine. We can't see the top and don't know how long it will take us to get there. When our path is uncertain and full of trials, it can be hard to be grateful.

But gratefulness is more than looking at the positives in life. Gratefulness is developing a sense of anticipation about the future. What is over this hill? What is coming for me around the bend? What is on the other side of this storm? Chances are it is a part of the adventure that will mold and shape us into who God wants us to be, but only if we allow it to do so.

Gratefulness is keeping our eyes searching for what God is doing in us and with us along life's road. It won't always be easy, but we can be grateful for the plans he has for us.

I don't have to chase extraordinary moments to find happiness—it's right in front of me if I'm paying attention and practicing gratitude.

Brené Brown

Gratitude unlocks the fullness of life. It turns what we have into enough, and more. It turns denial into acceptance, chaos to order, confusion to clarity. It can turn a meal into a feast, a house into a home, a stranger into a friend.

Melody Beattie

I would maintain that thanks are the highest form of thought; and that gratitude is happiness doubled by wonder.

G. K. Chesterton

For Further Reflection

Jeremiah 29:11; Psalm 118:24; Acts 24:3

TODAY'S PRAYER

God, forgive me for not recognizing all the blessings you have given me. Help me to walk today in gratitude. Amen.

Freedom on the Inside

If the Son sets you free, you will be free indeed.

JOHN 8:36

In 1995, Hollywood released *Braveheart*, a movie about the cost of fighting for freedom. The movie centered on a Scottish man who led his countrymen in a battle to have their own king and no longer be subject to England. Such freedom would affect how the Scottish managed their trade, their alliances, their finances, and ultimately their place in the world. The famous line at the end of the movie is the lead actor yelling "Freedom!" as he dies.

The freedom portrayed in the movie is honorable and noble, but it is also limited and focused on external things. The Bible talks about spiritual freedom that will transform us from the inside. We all live for something. For some people it's money, the next promotion, social or career status, health and fitness, a hobby or pleasure. We might try to justify why we "need" this thing we devote our lives to, but our single-minded drive for something—whether it be pleasure, comfort, or success—can become a form of bondage.

Christ's mission is to set us spiritually free from sin and whatever obstacles hinder our walk with him. The freedom he provides empowers us to live differently—as overcomers, even in the midst of the most challenging circumstances. Living in freedom can mean that even though we're going through tough times, we are open to serving others and obeying God's commands. Even though we do not feel our best, we listen and follow, playing an active role in the changes God wants to make in our hearts and lives.

From an earthly mind-set, it makes no sense to serve when we don't feel like it. But God has set us free with a purpose, so that we can do the tasks he has prepared for us.

Freedom lies in being bold.

Robert Frost

Peace doesn't come from finding a lake with no storms. It comes from having Jesus in the boat.

John Ortberg

For Further Reflection

Galatians 5:1; 1 Peter 2:16; Psalm 118:5

TODAY'S PRAYER

God, thank you for my liberty in Christ. Please help me to walk in it and use my freedom to serve others and do the work you've called me to. Amen.

The God of the Depressed

*One God and Father of all, who is over all
and through all and in all.*

EPHESIANS 4:6

God is sovereign and all powerful. He has no restrictions, no limits, and no need for assistance. Events detailed throughout Scripture demonstrate God's strength against his enemies, as well as his miraculous workings through the lives of his chosen people as they act in obedience and faith. From Enoch to Noah to Abraham—people stepped out in confidence, rooted in the knowledge that the Lord of Hosts is sovereign.

It can be difficult to walk in the same assurance as those heroes of faith. How do we know that God is really in control? We know because Hebrews 13:8 states that he is the same yesterday, today, and forever. The same God who acted with mighty power in the past is here with us in the present. With all the advancements and sophistication of our world today, God has remained the same. The same God who walked with the Israelites in their moments of disappointment and disbelief walks with us. The same God who healed then can heal today. He is still active and in full control of every situation.

Because we know his character, we know he will not allow us to be overtaken by anything. He governs over all things, including depression. Because he is in full control, we can lean into a peace that passes all understanding.

If there is one single molecule in this universe running around loose, totally free of God's sovereignty, then we have no guarantee that a single promise of God will ever be fulfilled.

R. C. Sproul

If there is one single reason why good people turn evil, it is because they fail to recognize God's ownership over their kingdom, their vocation, their resources, their abilities, and above all their lives.

Erwin W. Lutzer

That which should distinguish the suffering of believers from unbelievers is the confidence that our suffering is under the control of an all-powerful and all-loving God. Our suffering has meaning and purpose in God's eternal plan, and he brings or allows to come into our lives only that which is for his glory and our good.

Jerry Bridges

For Further Reflection

Hebrews 11:27; Ephesians 1:11; Colossians 1:16–17

TODAY'S PRAYER

Thank you for being Lord over all. Everything. Nothing is in existence without your say-so. Please help me to remember the truth of who you are and what you command. Amen.

A Sudden Change of Plans

*In their hearts humans plan their course,
but the LORD establishes their steps.*

PROVERBS 16:9 NIV

Some people are excited by change. Others cringe and resist. Those of us who are planners might balk at detours and interruptions. We are moving forward with life, making plans for the day, weekend, year—taking everything into account. Then suddenly there is an interruption. Maybe it's subtle or maybe it's as if we're doing a 180-degree turn. We can almost hear our internal GPS saying "recalculating, recalculating" and coming up with nothing. The GPS has no destination to lock on to. Neither do we.

If we find ourselves facing an unexpected change, we are in good company with some of the people in the Bible. Acts 9 tells of the conversion of Saul. Saul was a Jewish Roman citizen who actively persecuted believers. Christians feared him. He broke into their homes and imprisoned anyone he thought became followers of the way of Christ. His reputation preceded him.

But one day when Saul was on his way to arrest more Christians, he met God in a miraculous way and surrendered his life. In that moment, all his plans changed. In fact, the course of his whole life changed. He became a missionary for Christ and one of the most well-known converts to Christianity.

Sometimes our best-laid plans are interrupted by unpleasant events, and it can be easy to fight it. But when it is an interruption by God, it is best to adjust our GPS to match his destination, knowing that the changes God allows into our lives can work for our good if we surrender to him.

He came, not as a flash of light or as an unapproachable conqueror, but as one whose first cries were heard by a peasant girl and a sleepy carpenter. God tapped humanity on its collective shoulder, "Pardon me," he said, and eternity interrupted time, divinity interrupted carnality, and heaven interrupted the earth in the form of a baby. Christianity was born in one big heavenly interruption.

Max Lucado

The great thing, if one can, is to stop regarding all the unpleasant things as interruptions of one's "own," or "real" life. The truth is of course that what one calls the interruptions are precisely one's real life—the life God is sending one day by day.

C. S. Lewis

Conversion is the lifelong process of turning away from our plans and turning toward God's maddening, disruptive creativity.

M. Craig Barnes

For Further Reflection

James 4:10; Ecclesiastes 3:1; Proverbs 3:5-6

TODAY'S PRAYER

"God, interrupt whatever we are doing so that we can join you in what you're doing." —Frances Chan

Upside of the Downside

As for you, you meant evil against me, but God meant it for good in order to bring about this present outcome, that many people would be kept alive [as they are this day].

GENESIS 50:20 AMP

Sometimes God puts us on a trajectory we think will bring us joy. Other times we encounter detours and setbacks.

In Joseph's early years, he experienced one setback after another. His brothers were intensely jealous of him and sold him into slavery. He endured many years of imprisonment and separation from his family and homeland. After eleven years, Joseph interpreted dreams for Pharaoh's butler and baker. He hoped that such attention would improve his situation, but the baker died (as Joseph had told him would happen, based on the dream) and the butler, once released, quickly forgot about Joseph. Two years later, Joseph interpreted a dream for Pharaoh. After this event, Joseph got promoted. Nine years later, during an intense famine, Joseph's family came to Egypt for food, and eventually Joseph reunited with them.

Joseph ended up being instrumental in saving his family and the citizens of Egypt. But that was not Joseph's plan, nor his family's plan. As Joseph reflected on his life, he realized that his setbacks were God's way to provide and save his family.

When we face a difficult relationship, a job loss, a chronic mental health diagnosis, or any other setback, it's hard to see the upside. But our struggles have a higher purpose that brings spiritual blessing. As the book of James says, "Consider it pure joy ... whenever you face trials of many kinds, because you know that the testing of your faith produces perseverance (James 1:2–3).

Adapting to this perspective is not easy, but it is worthwhile. Trials can help shape us into the character of Christ. Trials can also teach us difficult lessons about ourselves that we might not learn any other way.

Setbacks have an upside; they fuel new dreams.

Dara Torres

When surrounded by the ashes of all that I once cherished, despite my best efforts I can find no room to be thankful. But standing there amidst endless ash I must remember that although the ashes surround me, God surrounds the ashes. And once that realization settles upon me, I am what I thought I could never be ... I am thankful for ashes.

Craig D. Lounsbrough

It's not how far you fall, it's how high you bounce that counts.

Zig Ziglar

For Further Reflection

Psalm 27:1; Ezra 4:1–24; Romans 8:28

TODAY'S PRAYER

God, my foresight is so limited. While my situation may look bleak, help me to remember that you have a plan you are working out for your glory and my betterment. Amen.

Unresolved Grief

The LORD is close to the brokenhearted
and saves those who are crushed in spirit.

PSALM 34:18

Negative emotions can be uncomfortable. As a result, we try to avoid or lessen the impact. We might watch TV, indulge in too many alcoholic beverages, overeat, or block the emotion. We might argue with God. These types of coping skills do not help the negative emotions go away—at least not long-term.

What would it be like to turn toward the negative emotion instead? What would it be like to acknowledge that the pain is there, we don't like it, and we don't know what to do? Such action would require the courage to look at the emotion and recognize a loss. Maybe our losses look like this:

-  Grieving the loss of relationships because our symptoms have pushed others away.

- Grieving the loss of a social life because we withdraw and stop doing the things we once looked forward to.

- Grieving the loss of our health because we can no longer do the things we used to be able to.

- Grieving the loss of control because we feel no closer to relief.

Feel the emotions. Name the loss. Jesus did. When he heard that Lazarus had died, he was moved by the tears of Mary and Martha. He knows grief. He knows sorrow. So, turn to him and cry. Go back to him again and again and lay your emotions before him. He will not turn us away. He will not dismiss our struggle. Instead he will meet us where we are and embrace us.

Embrace your grief. For there, your soul will grow.

Carl Jung

Grief is like the ocean, it comes in waves ebbing and flowing. Sometimes the water is calm, and sometimes it is overwhelming. All we can do is learn to swim.

Vicki Harrison

I'd rather walk with God and not have my questions answered than not walk with God and have my questions answered.

Rick Warren

For Further Reflection
Psalm 40:1-2; Psalm 88; Hebrews 4:15-16

TODAY'S PRAYER

Lord, I shy away from grief. I know grief is something that you experienced; therefore, you can empathize with what I feel. Help me to embrace my time of grief. Amen.

The Negative Spin

Set your minds on things that are above,
not on things that are on earth.

COLOSSIANS 3:2 ESV

When we're depressed, the sky is grayer, the flowers don't smell, nothing brings joy. As we try to live out our lives, everything is viewed through the lens of depression, making average disappointment seem disastrous. Depression can turn neutral events bad. For example: You call a friend. There is no answer, so you leave a message. A couple of days go by and you still haven't heard from your friend. Depression can turn that event into "I guess they don't like me anymore." However, there is no evidence that would lead you to that conclusion. There could be any number of reasons why your friend has not called.

Depressive thinking also brings with it extreme thinking. The depressive mind takes getting a bad grade on a test to "I will never get into college."

The antidote for the negative spin cycle is looking at the event realistically. Lean on your support system to help you see things as they really are so that you can respond in a practical way. It is only when you wear the right lens that you can see life for what it really is.

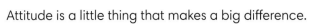

Attitude is a little thing that makes a big difference.

Winston Churchill

Attitude is more important than facts. It is more important than the past, than education, money, circumstances, than failures and success, than what other people think, say, or do. It is more important than appearance, ability, or skill. … The remarkable thing is I have a choice every day of what my attitude will be. … Life is ten percent what happens to me and ninety percent how I react to it.

Chuck Swindoll

We choose what attitudes we have right now. And it's a continuing choice.

John Maxwell

For Further Reflection

Jeremiah 17:9; 2 Corinthians 4:18; Isaiah 26:3

TODAY'S PRAYER

Lord, during these times, I admit my mind does not always think logically. Please help me to slow down and consider other possibilities. Please help me to remember others are willing to help. Amen.

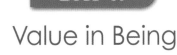

Value in Being

*But God shows his love for us in that while
we were still sinners, Christ died for us.*

ROMANS 5:8 ESV

We live in a world that values accomplishment. Our accomplishments are often rewarded in recognition, money, objects, or titles. Sometimes it can seem impossible to get anywhere without some proof of achievement—proof to the world that we are valuable.

What happens when, through no fault of our own, we can no longer "achieve"? What happens when our depression overtakes us to the point that completing basic household chores is a monumental feat?

From a practical standpoint, if the to-do list seems overwhelming, consider tackling it a different way:

- Don't clean the house, just take the trash out.
- Don't do all the laundry, just separate by color and pick one pile.
- Don't run all the errands, go to one store and pick up the necessities.

But if depression is leading to a self-esteem struggle and we find ourselves wondering if we are no longer a valued member of society, we must shove those lies aside and re-center on the truth: Because we are made in the image of God, we have value. God created our body, soul, and spirit with a care to detail greater than the most complex painting or the intricate parts of a leaf. God loves us with an unending, all-encompassing love.

The value of something is determined by the price that is paid. The price paid for us was Jesus' life. Setting aside all else, that fact alone sets upon us the highest value imaginable. We are valuable because God chose to make us so.

No one can make you feel inferior without your consent.

Eleanor Roosevelt

We are what we believe we are.

C. S. Lewis

Never bend your head. Always hold it high. Look the world straight in the face.

Helen Keller

For Further Reflection

Psalm 139:13–16; Ephesians 2:4–9; 1 Corinthians 6:20

TODAY'S PRAYER

"Lord, when I feel that what I'm doing is insignificant and unimportant, help me to remember that everything I do is significant and important in your eyes, because you love me and you put me here, and no one else can do what I am doing in exactly the way I do it." —Brennan Manning

Do the Opposite

*And be continually renewed in the spirit
of your mind [having a fresh, untarnished
mental and spiritual attitude].*

EPHESIANS 4:23 AMP

The emotions that accompany depression can be strong. They drive our behaviors and our thoughts and can have long-term effects. Whether we realize it or not, sometimes our emotions are in the driver's seat.

In the field of mental health, there are many tools and techniques to help those who struggle with depression, and one of those techniques is to do the opposite of what we feel inclined to do. Here is how it could work:

- Feel like staying in bed? Choose to get up and take a shower. Choose to get dressed in street clothes instead of pajamas.

- Feel like isolating? Choose to actively reach out to someone in your support circle, or take an interest in someone else. Maybe it's time to go somewhere where there are people, such as church or the park.

- Feel like sleeping? Choose to get active. Take a walk. Read a book. Call a friend and engage in conversation.

When we recognize that a behavior or emotion is getting in the way of us living a full and meaningful life, we can take steps to change. It sounds simple, but when we struggle with feelings of sadness and would rather withdraw into ourselves, that is the time to do the opposite. By doing so, we are choosing to change our experience, not suppress it. When we realize an emotion or behavior affects us negatively, we can choose to act in a way that produces a positive result instead.

God grant me the serenity to accept the things I cannot change, the courage to change the things I can, and the wisdom to know the difference.

Reinhold Niebuhr

To change a habit, make a conscious decision, then act out the new behavior.

Maxwell Maltz

We change our behavior when the pain of staying the same becomes greater than the pain of changing. Consequences give us the pain that motivates us to change.

Dr. Henry Cloud and Dr. John Townsend

For Further Reflection

Proverbs 15:18; Proverbs 29:11; Galatians 5:16–24

TODAY'S PRAYER

Lord, I get stuck in a rut following my feelings. When it is in my best interest and according to your will, please help me to make a different choice. In Jesus' name. Amen

Healing for the Broken

*The Spirit of the Sovereign LORD is on me, because the
LORD has anointed me to proclaim good news to the
poor. He has sent me to bind up the brokenhearted,
to proclaim freedom for the captives and release
from darkness for the prisoners.*

ISAIAH 61:1

Brokenness can mean many things. It can be a dish that fell on the floor. It can be something not working properly. It can be a loss for the zest of life, when we cannot get out of bed because we don't see the point. Depression can feel like we are broken, and it's a brokenness that can be hard to describe. All we know is that we are not ourselves. Even though we cannot always articulate what is happening inside us, God knows where to meet us.

In the Old Testament, the prophet Isaiah was called into service just as the Assyrian Empire began to expand, which was a threat to Israel. As Israel recognized this growing threat, they became fearful and distraught. God sent Isaiah to give them words of encouragement. In the New Testament, Jesus read Isaiah 61:1-2 at the synagogue in Nazareth and told the people "Today this scripture is fulfilled in your hearing" (Luke 4:21), meaning he was the fulfillment of that prophecy.

The Lord wanted to comfort his people when they were facing a physical threat, but he is also there to help with our emotional wounds. When God puts into motion a plan for healing, we experience the gift of "beauty instead of ashes, the oil of joy instead of mourning, and a garment of praise instead of a spirit of despair" (Isaiah 61:3).

All of us have broken areas of our lives. But God is our great comforter and healer, and he can bring the deep emotional healing that leads to hope and new life.

Do not grudge the Hand that is molding the still too shapeless image within you. It is growing more beautiful, though you see it not, and every touch of temptation may add to its perfection.

Henry Drummord

When God is involved, anything can happen. Be open. Stay that way. God has a beautiful way of bringing good vibrations out of broken chords.

Chuck Swindoll

We will stand amazed to see the topside of the tapestry and how God beautifully embroidered each circumstance into a pattern for our good and his glory.

Joni Eareckson Tada

For Further Reflection
Luke 4:16–22; Psalm 46:1–3; Isaiah 61:1–3

TODAY'S PRAYER

Lord, I bring you all my broken pieces and leave them in your hands, trusting that you will put me back together in a way that brings you glory. Amen.

Big Enough Hands

*Who has measured the waters in the hollow of his hand,
or with the breadth of his hand marked off the heavens?
Who has held the dust of the earth in a basket,
or weighed the mountains on the scales
and the hills in a balance?*

Isaiah 40:12

Children have the best imagination! They believe they have superpowers and can save the world. They are amazed at the simplest things—like rain. They are not thinking about where it comes from. They want to taste it. They want to catch it with their bare hands, even though that's impossible. Try as they might, the water leaks between their fingers or overflows their cupped hands and hits the ground.

Sometimes life can feel like trying to catch rain. Trying to manage the everyday challenges and schedules can seem futile or overwhelming. Sometimes things we hadn't planned are added to our plates. We try to balance and adjust, but no matter how hard we try, our hands cannot hold it all. With the addition of a chronic sadness such as depression, our skills at managing life can dwindle and other pieces of life slip through our fingers.

Scripture brings us comfort, reassuring us repeatedly that nothing slips past God. God knows us intimately. He knows when things are going well and when we are sick in our soul. He knows us better than our closest friend does. He knows us better than we know ourselves. And because he is all powerful and all knowing, he doesn't lose track of anything.

When our lives are poured into his hands, nothing slips through his fingers.

We cannot begin to define God's knowledge. We know, simply and profoundly, that nothing is hidden from him or incomprehensible to him.

Elizabeth George

Man has to start with something and then develop it—he cannot ever make anything from nothing, only God can do that and call forth the creation.

Margaret Weston

For Further Reflection

Psalm 139:6; 1 John 3:20; Job 37:16

TODAY'S PRAYER

I put my hand in yours, Lord, trusting you. May I always remember that you are big enough to manage my life and everything that comes my way. Amen.

Reignited for Joy

Therefore you now have sorrow. But I will see you again,
and your heart will rejoice, and no one
will take your joy from you.

JOHN 16:22 MEV

If we struggle with depression, joy might not be at the forefront of our minds. Well-meaning friends might even go as far as to say that if the person experiencing depression would "just get out and do something, they will feel better." However, it's not that easy. We probably know that getting out and socializing might help lift our mood. At the same time, the symptoms of depression prevent us from being motivated to reach out and participate in joyful events.

To help reignite joy in our lives, we can remember some old truths. First, true joy comes from God. In Christ, we have a joy that cannot be taken away. Because God is ever present with us, we can always embrace the joy that comes from him.

Second, as Psalm 30:5 says, "weeping may stay for the night, but rejoicing comes in the morning." No matter how much pain or worry we are experiencing, we can be comforted and encouraged with the truth that there is a season for everything, including joy.

Third, we can rejoice in the knowledge that God hears us. The Bible is full of examples of times when God's people called to him and he answered. We can experience an abiding joy that is not dependent on our temporary circumstances, a joy that can help us persevere through them.

Admittedly, when we're in the middle of depressive symptoms it can be difficult to remember that we have God, the source of all joy, with us. But we can be intentional in remembering that his mercies are new each day, which means each morning offers the opportunity for joy, despite our circumstances.

Joy is the serious business of Heaven.

C. S. Lewis

Joy does not simply happen to us. We have to choose joy and keep choosing it every day.

Henri Nouwen

For Further Reflection

Habakkuk 3:17–18; Psalm 30:5; Romans 15:13

TODAY'S PRAYER

Father, as long as I am on earth, I know that adversities will come and go. As I take each step, please help me remember to choose joy. Amen.

Anchors in the Storm

We have this as a sure and steadfast anchor
of the soul, a hope that enters into the inner
place behind the curtain.

HEBREWS 6:19 ESV

Along the Atlantic and Gulf Coasts of the United States, hurricanes are part of the environment. The heavy winds, downpours, and occasional tornadoes that hurricanes bring can cause great damage. Hurricanes have the power to tear roofs off buildings, knock down trees and power lines, and flood major streets. Whenever possible, people will pull their boats from the sea in advance of the storm. But in some cases, a boat stays in the water with an anchor that prevents it from being tossed around in the ocean. When that anchor is secure, not even the strongest currents can move the boat.

We need anchors in our lives. Even when things appear calm on the surface, we can be drifting from God without realizing it. For believers, our anchors are God and his promises. We need these anchors for three reasons: (1) There will be storms. Hardship will come. Whether the storm is a job loss, a sickness or any number of difficulties we face, we need to be rooted securely so that we will not be tossed by the current. (2) We tend to drift. If we are honest with ourselves, the events in our world can shift our understanding of who God is. As we shift, we are either moving toward God or away from him. (3) We pick easy relief. Persevering through hardship is hard work. We can be tempted to take the easy route, which can take different forms—a relationship, a quick symptom-reliever, or the latest fad.

In the turbulence of life, we need anchors to root us in truth, hope, and peace. God will be our strength when we feel we cannot hold on, and his promises are sure and steadfast.

Without Christ there is no hope.

Charles Spurgeon

If your faith isn't rooted in the Bible, it will wither like a plant pulled out of the soil.

Billy Graham

Faith is like a tender plant, rooted in Christ alone, watered by the Spirit and the Word, strengthened by the winds of adversity and the sunshine of blessing.

Anne Graham Lotz

For Further Reflection

Psalm 42:11; Isaiah 26:3; Isaiah 28:16

TODAY'S PRAYER

Lord, thank you for being my anchor in times of trouble. I praise you for never shifting or changing. Please help me to remember to stay rooted in you.

Amen.

DAY 95

Forgiveness

Judge not, and you will not be judged;
condemn not, and you will not be condemned;
forgive, and you will be forgiven.

LUKE 6:37 ESV

One of the main topics of the Bible is forgiveness. The same God who forgives our sins wants us to forgive others and surrender our hurts to him. By doing so, we will begin to heal not only our hearts but also our bodies. Whether it is a small disagreement, an argument that comes from betrayal, or the harm someone inflicted upon us, unresolved hurt can affect us physically. Forgiving someone who harmed us is as much for our benefit as for the person who wronged us.

For believers, forgiveness is more than just saying the words. It is the conscious decision to no longer hold on to the harm the other person inflicted on you. It is not denying pain or the wrongdoing. It is the deliberate act of turning the situation over to God.

According to Dr. Karen Swartz of Johns Hopkins Medicine, longstanding anger and unresolved conflict affects our bodies by constantly changing our heart rate, blood pressure, and stress levels. Constant changes in these two areas can lead to an increase in depression and heart disease.[11] However, the regular practice of forgiveness and turning hurts over to God can lower our stress levels and improve our health.

The journey to forgiveness is not an easy one. Though we believe we have forgiven, at times the pain might resurface. Forgive again. God would not command us to forgive if it were not possible, and he will provide the strength when we don't think we can do it.

To forgive is to set a prisoner free and discover that the prisoner was you.

Lewis B. Smedes

Forgiveness is the fragrance that the violet sheds on the heel that has crushed it.

Mark Twain

Forgiveness says you are given another chance to make a new beginning.

Desmond Tutu

For Further Reflection

Ephesians 4:32; 1 John 1:9; Colossians 3:13

TODAY'S PRAYER

Lord, please search me and reveal any areas of unforgiveness in my life. Help me to always lead with forgiveness and love, the same way you have forgiven and loved me. Amen.

Spiritual Warfare Is Real

No temptation has overtaken you that is not common to man. God is faithful, and he will not let you be tempted beyond your ability, but with the temptation he will also provide the way of escape, that you may be able to endure it.

1 CORINTHIANS 10:13 ESV

Maybe we thought we had it all together. Then one day those moments of joy and productivity end. For whatever reason, we have become overwhelmed with despondency and hopelessness. The days of looking ahead with anticipation are gone, replaced by dread as soon as we open our eyes. We want to be with family and friends, to feel like our old selves again, but the thought of engaging in any of those things is exhausting. We receive excellent medical care and follow all the recommendations for integrating friends and family into our lives. But something is still missing.

In some cases, depression isn't rooted in the physical or the emotional but rather the spiritual. We must ask the Lord to show us truth, and in so doing, we might discover false beliefs or lies that have affected our choices and way of thinking.

Satan is an opportunist. He knows where we struggle and will use those weaknesses in any way he can to move us in a direction that is opposite what God has for us. Scripture tells us he has been sneaky since the beginning of time. He put his tricks into motion with the fist humans by asking Eve, "Did God actually say...?" Satan does the same today. He is subtle. He knows just when and how to attack to do the most damage.

While we work to find the root of our depressive symptoms, we should ask God to reveal any lie or half-truth that might be driving our lives and replace it with the truths of Scripture.

Self-rejection is the greatest enemy of the spiritual life because it contradicts the sacred voice that calls us the "Beloved." Being the Beloved constitutes the core truth of our existence.

Henri Nouwen

The nature of the enemy's warfare in your life is to cause you to become discouraged and to cast away your confidence. … The enemy wants to numb you into a coping kind of Christianity that has given up hope of seeing God's resurrection power.

Bob Sorge

Spiritual warfare is very real. There is a furious, fierce, and ferocious battle raging in the realm of the spirit between the forces of God and the forces of evil. Warfare happens every day, all the time. Whether you believe it or not, you are in a battlefield.

Pedro Okoro

For Further Reflection
Psalm 51:12; Ephesians 6:11–12; 1 Peter 5:8

TODAY'S PRAYER

Father, thank you for the reminder that sometimes the fight has nothing to do with my body or mind but rather an attack from the enemy. Help me to use the words of God to bring every thought captive. Amen.

Making Lemonade

*This is the day the L*ORD *has made;*
We will rejoice and be glad in it.

PSALM 118:24 NKJV

Maybe you are familiar with this saying: *When life gives you lemons, make lemonade.* Pretty simple, but let's take a deeper look. Lemons are in fact sour, tart and are often used sparingly in purest form. However, coupled with one or two other ingredients, lemons turn into a flavorful drink that can be used to quench thirst on a hot day. That same tartness can be blended with even more ingredients and we now have a dessert that wins the prize at the local fair. But at its core, a lemon is still the tart, cringe-worthy piece of fruit.

There are times when—as the saying goes—life give us lemons. We come face to face with challenges or periods of difficulty that seem to come out of nowhere and may seem endless. It can be easy to pour all our time and energy into trying to figure out how we got the lemon, why we got the lemon or what to do with the lemon. These questions are good, but at the end of the day, we still have the lemons.

Perhaps a better way to cope with the tartness of life is to embrace it. We can do this by looking around and seeing what we can do with that challenge or difficulty. Addressing some of the original questions about the lemons can show an opportunity to invest in relationships that have not always been a priority. Looking at ourselves could provide a good time to look at our diet and overall health.

We never know what life will bring us. And Jesus did say in John 16:33 that we will have trouble. But he also tells us to cheer up because he has already overcome any struggle that we may have. It's a fact! And no one can make lemonade like Jesus.

Dwell on the beauty of life. Watch the stars, and see yourself running with them.

Marcus Aurelius

The essence of optimism is that it takes no account of the present, but it is a source of inspiration, of vitality and hope where others have resigned; it enables a man to hold his head high, to claim the future for himself and not to abandon it to his enemy.

Dietrich Bonhoeffer

Sometimes when you're in a dark place you think you've been buried, but you've actually been planted.

Christine Caine

For Further Reflection

Philippians 4:12; Romans 8:25; Psalm 43:5

TODAY'S PRAYER

God, I just want to thank you that with your help I can change my sadness into dancing. I know it doesn't mean all is fixed but I do know that with you there is always a hope. Please help me to remember that. Amen.

DAY 98

Knowing God

What may be known about God is plain to them,
because God has made it plain to them.

ROMANS 1:19 NIV

The amount of information we take in daily is incalculable. What we see, hear, smell, taste, touch with our fingers—anything we experience—is all being interpreted and logged into our brains. We typically do not have to think too much about familiar experiences and how to translate them. However, when something new comes into our lives, it can throw us off. We can start to try to make sense of it by trying to develop a new interpretation (not knowing until much later if that interpretation is true) or, in the moment, we can recall what we already know to be true and use that lens to help us navigate the new experience.

Sometimes this can explain what happens to us when we have a negative encounter in life. The event surprises us. We stumble to figure it out, figure out our next step—coming up with thoughts or ideas that could be distorted, misleading, or false. While we are spinning to make sense of it all, we forgot what we already know. We have forgotten the foundation that has offered us hope in all situations. And that hope is knowing God.

We can all admit that we don't know everything about life or everything about God, but we do know some things. One thing we do know is that he is a loving God that never changes. If we remember nothing else, we can approach any situation in life through this lens and know that God loves us. In our approach, we have the opportunity to learn even more about God and his ways. And because he loves us, he will do what is best for us. It may not immediately solve the problem, but with a lens of love we can persevere.

Once you become aware that the main business that you are here for is to know God, most of life's problems fall into place of their own accord.

J. I. Packer

But to enjoy him we must know him. Seeing is savoring. If he remains a blurry, vague fog, we may be intrigued for a season. But we will not be stunned with joy, as when the fog clears and you find yourself on the brink of some vast precipice.

John Piper

Bible study without Bible experience is pointless. Knowing Psalm 23 is different from knowing the shepherd.

Kingsley Opuwari Manuel

Further Reflection
Psalm 119:160; Psalm 25:5; John 1:14

TODAY'S PRAYER

Lord, I pray you help me to accept the truth of what you want me to experience and leave the rest behind. Please help me to be aware of when I start to develop my own truth and submit them to you.
In Jesus' name. Amen.

Dangerous Shortcuts

*Also it is not good for a person to be without knowledge,
and he who hurries with his feet [acting impulsively
and proceeding without caution or analyzing the
consequences] sins (misses the mark).*

PROVERBS 19:2 AMP

We all experience the ups and downs of life. For some events, we just ride the roller coaster. We are able to navigate the path to some sense of relief or normalcy, adapting easily to whatever comes our way. In the end, we recover quickly and proceed with life. For other life events, the ups and downs of life can be disruptive. This can be in the form of a loss, grief, sadness, and even anger. We ride it out, sometimes reluctantly, but we can admit that we just want to get to the end no matter what it takes.

While it might be tempting to avoid negative experiences or to quickly move through the unpleasant emotions, doing so can lead to more danger than good. Quick fixes might get us from point A to point B or provide a quick reprieve from what ails us. After a while, we might feel better. But if we never get to the root of what could be causing the disruptions or what is causing the negative feelings, we are only addressing symptoms.

When it comes to living our best life, we want to take the best route, which might mean a longer road. It is not enough to scratch the surface and address warning signs. We must be willing to dive deep into areas we may have ignored or forgotten about. To experience healing, we must be willing to consider the road that brought us to this point.

Taking a shortcut might seem like a good idea, but it is not always the best strategy. Similarly, following Christ might include traveling roads and taking detours that are not pleasant in the moment but are better for us in the long run.

You always reap what you sow; there is no shortcut.

Stephen Covey

You may encounter many defeats, but you must not be defeated. In fact, it may be necessary to encounter the defeats, so you can know who you are, what you can rise from, how you can still come out of it.

Maya Angelou

It's not that I'm so smart, it's just that I stay with problems longer.

Albert Einstein

For Further Reflection

Psalm 32:8; Psalm 37:7; James 1:4

TODAY'S PRAYER

Father, I am tired, and I just want relief. I am tempted to take shortcuts, but I know that's not the best strategy. Please help me to stay the course. Amen.

The Gift of Hope

*May the God of hope fill you with all joy and peace
as you trust in him, so that you may overflow
with hope by the power of the Holy Spirit.*

Romans 15:13

A chronic ailment can certainly change our outlook on life and perspective about the future. We might spend most of our energy simply managing today. With depressive symptoms, getting out of bed might be all we set our sights on. But even in the smallest of efforts, like getting out of bed, there is an element of hope.

Hope is a small but powerful word. For the believer in Christ, hope is the expectation that God will make something happen. Sometimes hope gets put in the category of an emotion or a wish. But biblical hope is a confident assurance—a decision to believe in God's promises, even when our circumstances look hopeless.

It might seem contradictory to think that in the midst of an illness or loss we could have hope. But because God said he will supply all our needs (Philippians 4:19), we can rest in the expectation that he will provide and he is working everything for his divine purposes. Our hope is in God, who does not lie or change. He sees and knows all things. Nothing is out of his control or impossible for him.

During difficult times, we will be tempted to lose our hope that anything will ever change. When those thoughts come to mind, reflect on the thousands of instances in the Bible where God did what he said he would do. We will see examples of his faithfulness to his promises and know he will continue to be faithful. Our hope is on solid ground.

The very least you can do in your life is figure out what you hope for. And the most you can do is live inside that hope. Not admire it from a distance but live right in it, under its roof.

Barbara Kingsolver

We must accept finite disappointment, but never lose infinite hope.

Martin Luther King, Jr.

For Further Reflection

Job 11:18-19; Isaiah 40:31; Proverb 23:18

TODAY'S PRAYER

Father, from this point forward, please help me to keep my hope in you—not in people or things but in the one who created everything. Thank you for your promises and for new mercy every day. Amen.

Endnotes

1   "Depression." Last updated February 2018. National Institute of Mental Health: *https://www.nimh.nih.gov/health/topics/depression/index.shtml.*

2   Caryl-Sue, National Geographic Society, "Cast-Net Fishing." Last updated January 9, 2012. National Geographic: *https://www.nationalgeographic.org/media/cast-net.*

3   Inagaki, T. K., Bryne Haltom, K. E., Suzuki, S., Jevtic, I., Hornstein, E., Bower, J. E., & Eisenberger, N. I. (2016). "The Neurobiology of Giving Versus Receiving Support: The Role of Stress-Related and Social Reward-Related Neural Activity," *Psychosomatic Medicine: Journal of Biobehavioral Medicine*, 78(4): 443–453.

4   House, J. S., Landis, K. R., Umberston, D. (1988). "Social Relationships and Health," Science, 241(4865): 540–545.

5   Salimpoor, V. N., Benovoy, M., Larcher, K., Dagher, A., & Zatorre, R. J. (2011). "Anatomically distinct dopamine release during anticipation and experience of peak emotion to music." Nature neuroscience, 14(2): 257–262.

6   "Stress Symptoms: Effects on your body and behavior," Mayo Clinic: *https://www.mayoclinic.org/healthy-lifestyle/stress-management/in-depth/stress-symptoms/art-20050987* (Retrieved September 17, 2020).

7   Jessie Szalay, "Giant Sequoias and Redwoods: The Largest and Tallest Trees," LiveScience. May 5, 2017. *https://www.livescience.com.*

8   Dictionary.com, s. v. "remember." *www.dictionary.com.*

9   Katherine Zeratsky, "Junk food blues: Are depression and diet related?" Mayo Clinic: *https://www.mayoclinic.org/diseases-conditions/depression/expert-answers/depression-and-diet/faq-20058241* (Retrieved September 23, 2020).

10 "What is the Mediterranean Diet?" January 9, 2020. American Heart Association: *https://www.heart.org/en/healthy-living/healthy-eating/eat-smart/nutrition-basics/mediterranean-diet*; "Take Your Diet to the Mediterranean," Johns Hopkins Medicine: *https://www.hopkinsmedicine.org/health/wellness-and-prevention/take-your-diet-to-the-mediterranean* (Retrieved November 1, 2020).

11 "Forgiveness: Your health depends on it," Johns Hopkins Medicine: *https://www.hopkinsmedicine.org/health/wellness-and-prevention/forgiveness-your-health-depends-on-it* (Retrieved October 5, 2020).